TROUBLED
waters

RUTH BALINT studied history at the University of Sydney, before going on to make the film *Troubled Waters*, which was the catalyst for this book. The film won the Dendy Best Documentary award in 2002. After the completion of her PhD in history, she worked as a video-journalist and producer for the SBS *Insight* program. She is currently a lecturer in the School of History at the University of New South Wales. Ruth lives in Sydney and counts Broome as her second home.

TROUBLED
waters

*Borders, boundaries and possession
in the Timor Sea*

RUTH BALINT

ALLEN&UNWIN

Allen & Unwin
83 Alexander Street
Crows Nest NSW 2065
Australia
Phone: (61 2) 8425 0100
Fax: (61 2) 9906 2218
Email: info@allenandunwin.com
Web: www.allenandunwin.com

National Library of Australia
Cataloguing-in-Publication entry:

Balint, Ruth.
    Troubled waters: Borders, boundaries and possession in the Timor Sea.

    Bibliography.
    Includes index.
    ISBN 1 74114 361 6.

    1. Fishers—Timor Island. 2. Territorial waters—
    Australia. 3. Timor Island—History. 4. Timor Island—
    Social life and customs. 5. Timor Island—Politics and
    government. 6. Timor Sea. I. Title.

959.86

Set in 11/13pt Bembo by Asset Typesetting Pty Ltd
Printed in Australia by McPherson's Printing Group

10 9 8 7 6 5 4 3 2 1

For my parents, Eva and Tony
For everything

And in memory of
Johni Fakie, 1976–2004

CONTENTS

ACKNOWLEDGMENTS

I AM DEEPLY indebted to the fishermen of
Pepela, Rote for sharing their stories with me. They were
enormously generous with their time, thoughts and homes. I
hope I have used their words justly and with the respect they
deserve. Thanks go especially to Sadli Hudari Ardani, Abdul
Gani Pello, Johni Fakie, Agung Prasata, Peter Isak Husein, Haji
Hasan and Matteos Tungga, who gave me their experiences
and ideas and told me everything about the traditional
fishermen's world. Their words are the poetry in this book.

This book was first a documentary film. Many of the
interviews used here came from the making of *Troubled
Waters*. In May 2001, I flew to Indonesia with Max Bourke,
and travelled to the fishing village of Pepela in Rote. In
Pepela, Haji Hasan, our host, walked us to the police hut on
the outskirts of the village. The police chief gave us permission to film, despite his knowledge that we had been
forbidden to by the Indonesian government. For that I am
eternally grateful.

Max and I were only in Pepela for ten days. Because of
the risks associated with our visa status, we didn't do much
labelling or keep notes. Therefore, the interviews conducted

during this time are undated. They were conducted between 20 and 30 May 2001. Other interviews conducted with the fishermen in Australian jails are dated.

Thank you to Joanne McGowan of Resonance Productions who was the producer of the film and had faith in it from the start. Also to John Hughes of SBS Independent for showing the first interest. The Film Finance Corporation Australia assisted with finance for the film, and thanks goes to Susan MacKinnon. Sue Piper did a wonderful job of transcribing all the interviews, with help from Budi Herbinobowo and Abbie Messiter. Many of their translations did not make it into the film but have appeared here. Thank you most of all to Max Bourke for being an amazing, intrepid cameraman and a wonderful friend. Finally, on the subject of filming, thank you to executive producer Mike Carey, who commissioned my report, 'The Death of Mansur' for the SBS program *Insight* in 2003, and executive producer Mark Maley who oversaw its television debut. Some of the material I gathered for that story has made it into this book.

Mina Sarubin gave me my first opportunity to meet the Indonesian fishermen in Australia, and acted as an interpreter in all my early conversations. Without Mina, I would never have started on this journey. Thank you to my first Indonesian fisherman friend La Bau Wajo.

After it was a film, it became a History PhD thesis. My PhD supervisor Richard Waterhouse's comments and advice were invaluable. He gave me enormous encouragement in my work, and I am especially grateful to Richard for his enthusiasm about my topic, and for reading this manuscript before publication. David Walker, Kirsten McKenzie and Ann Curthoys all read my original thesis and gave me valuable advice. Thanks goes also to Richard White for his ongoing support and to Jan Kociumbas whose teaching first inspired, then nurtured, my love of Australian history.

There were a number of people who greatly assisted me with research, both in Australia and in Indonesia. Tom Therik from the Universitas Kristas guided me in Kupang, West Timor. I thank Western Australian Fisheries, especially Mike O'Dea, Tom Morris, Mick Flanagan and Chris Mitchell for their assistance. A special thank you also to Jill Elliot and Frank Harkin, and to Ted Wilkinson and Philip Vincent, who have all had lengthy personal involvement with the traditional Indonesian fishermen incarcerated in WA jails.

I am especially grateful to Dan Dwyer, who supported me on numerous occasions in Darwin and who read and commented on parts of the book. He knows far more than me about traditional Indonesian fishing. Thanks to Natasha Stacey, Gus Bottrill and Maxine Chi for their generosity with their own research. In Broome, a number of people gave me oral history interviews. A very special thank you to Carol Tang Wei, Peter Matsumoto, Mick Manolis, Georgina Kaissis, Maxine Chi, Sherena Bin Hitam, Vanessa Poelina, and Irene and Eric Hunter from One Arm Point Aboriginal Community. Some of their incredible histories have made it into this book.

The PhD thesis was the manuscript for this book. I must thank the judges of the Vogel for awarding me this prestigious prize in 2003, which has led to this publication. Thank you Stella Clarke, Jean Bedford, James Bradley and Andrew Riemer — I am deeply honoured. At Allen & Unwin, senior publisher Annette Barlow, my editor Christa Munns, April Murdoch and all the team that helped get this to book form, my heartfelt gratitude. Thanks also to Sue Grose-Hodge for the fine editing, it couldn't have come sooner.

Finally, there are some people who have suffered through all of *Troubled Waters*' manifestations. My father painstakingly read and edited every draft chapter of the PhD thesis. My mother's encouragement and support saw me through.

My brothers Kali and Dan backed me every step of the way. Roger was amazing. No-one will be more relieved than my grandma Magdi that this is finally a book. My grandparents Evi and Imre are no longer here but are always in my thoughts. The rest of the family are too numerous to mention, but are not forgotten. A very special thank you to Ron Brookes. To Arini, Yahya, Johnny and all my close friends: Phew!

Finally, to Edi, Boba and Aki, for always being there. I couldn't have done it without you. Thank you for all the listening.

Northern Australia and the islands and reefs in the Timor Sea

PROLOGUE

THE SIX MEN in the fishing boat spot the Australian warship in the grey light of dawn. The evening before, a low drone warning of its approach, an Australian surveillance plane materialised in the skies above them, circling once, twice, before arcing away. The sound of its engines lingered in the evening air long after it disappeared from view. That night, lying head to toe in the little six-foot cabin, they spend a restless night, wondering whether their boat has drifted out of the legal limits. They are sure they have stayed within them, but perhaps the current has carried them to other waters. It has happened before.

The ship is still some distance away. The fishermen quickly let out their sails and point their boat northwest, cursing the direction of the wind. The wind is mild but, forced to tack into it, their progress is slow. They argue whether they should throw the catch overboard. A month of backbreaking work and at least six months of their families' livelihoods rests in that one catch. In the end, their voices trail off. The five younger men watch the old man watch the warship loom larger, and wait for him to decide.

Hours pass. The distance between the two boats lessens, not lengthens. The fishermen can almost hear the laughter of the naval vessel leisurely closing the gap as their own tiny craft struggles to maintain its exhausting pace. Loudspeakers boom out over the water, commanding them to halt. A rubber dinghy is lowered into the water, followed by five officers. Within minutes, the Australians are alongside, three of them clambering on board the 10-metre fishing boat. There isn't room for more. It lurches dangerously under the extra weight.

'Juragan? Captain?' The old man is separated from the others, who are herded to the foredeck. One of the officers, an Australian Fisheries inspector, asks for the captain's papers. He holds up an Indonesian language card. 'Where are you from?' he reads aloud. The old man points to the compass, the sky and the sea, his speech urgent, insistent. The two naval officers who have climbed aboard guard the other five fishermen. They are not interested in these preliminaries. They already have the coordinates placing the boat inside the Australian Fishing Zone, and the stench of drying fish carcasses has been blowing in their faces all day.

The fishermen become distressed when it is clear they are going to be arrested. The officers respond forcefully and by early evening, the Australian patrol vessel is on its way to Broome. The six fishermen remain with their boat, furiously pumping water as the Australian ship tows it behind. But in the end, the speed of the tow is too much for her. By 10 p.m. water is coming in fast. Defeated, the fishermen ride the rest of the journey facing backwards on the deck of the naval vessel, watching their boat break up under the strain.

INTRODUCTION

> You must have plenty of sea-room to tell the
> Truth in.
>
> —Herman Melville, *Moby Dick*

A YOUNG ROTENESE fisherman picks up a stick and begins to draw a map in the sand. 'This is where Rote Island is located and to its south is Pulau Pasir,' Gani Pello says, the stick perfectly tracing the three crooked shapes that make up what Australians know as Ashmore Reef. The shapes of other reefs — Cartier, Seringapatam, Scott — follow, their Indonesian names too quick for me to catch. A huddle of children watch on and as his map becomes more detailed, Gani teaches them how to sail there too. 'At night we use stars to give us direction.' Gani sketches the sky. Winds and currents are woven into the story, together transforming Gani's canvas into a theatre of voyaging that encompasses the oceans of his father, grandfather and all the seafarers of his ancestry. The oil rigs in the Timor Sea make it the modern seascape of his lifetime as well.

We are standing on the beach in Pepela, a fishing village on the southeast coast of the island of Rote.[1] Rote is in the

Nusa Tenggara region of Indonesia, just south of West Timor. I am there to make a documentary film about the impact of the expansion of Australia's maritime borders on the traditional fishermen of this tiny fishing village. For me, the route to Pepela has been fraught with endless obstacles and bureaucratic red tape. But for Gani, the journey has taken much longer. He has been back in Pepela only a month, after spending sixteen months in Australian prisons and another four weeks finding his way home.

I had first met Gani two months before. My intention had been to interview him while he was in prison, and to follow his story from there. I knew that he was due for release soon. But getting access to Indonesian fishermen in jail as a filmmaker proved impossible. On the day that I heard he had been transported from prison to the immigration detention centre at Perth airport pending his repatriation to Denpasar in Indonesia, I decided to chance a visit. The plan was risky. I wasn't even sure whether he would still be there, and even if he were, Gani had never seen or heard of me. The only visitors allowed were friends and relatives, and visits had to be requested by the prisoner. With my friends waiting in the car, I went in alone. Somehow, after jumping through all the security hoops, I was admitted to the visitors' room. The guard had gone to talk to Gani and he had, miraculously, verified our acquaintance.

A couple sat in a corner, a young Australian woman like myself saying a teary farewell to another male deportee. When Gani was escorted into the room, he played along beautifully. No one watching, neither the officer standing guard nor those monitoring the surveillance cameras positioned around the ceiling, would have guessed we were anything but old friends. *Please, tell me my family is OK*, he had whispered urgently, imagining that I was the bearer of ill-tidings. Sadly, bad news from home is a common enough experience for the dozens of

Indonesian fishermen regularly locked up in Australian jails. *I am coming to Pepela*, I said, telling him quickly of the film. Two months later, I finally arrived. Gani was there to meet me as I stepped off the ferry.

Now, watching him on the beach, his face no longer strained with the trauma of imprisonment, absorbed in the creation of this richly detailed tapestry in the sand, I thought about this sea that had bound the fates of Rotenese fishermen like Gani so closely to Australia. The sea Gani was drawing had virtually nothing in common with the Timor Sea of Australian imagining. Gani's sea was a familiar, intimate place, the construct of a fisherman who knows the elaborate characteristics of its territory in much the same way as a gardener might know the special curves of a garden, the places of its unevenness, the way the wind whistles through the trees at a certain time of year. It brought alive what would appear, to an earthbound stranger like myself, an empty, featureless expanse of water. But for the vast majority of Australians, the Timor Sea is viewed as neither a welcoming nor a benign place. It has come to represent a sort of tyranny in the national psyche, a bleak sea associated with the threat of alien invasion and the vulnerability of the nation's sovereignty. It is the image of desperate people in decrepit, rotting boats, the artillery of guns and ships and the language of disaster — 'flood', 'tidal wave' and 'tsunami' — that nowadays epitomises Australia's Timor Sea.

Finally, Gani tapped a large craggy rock that now sat at the head of the sand map. Australia. 'As far as the border between Australia and Indonesia is concerned,' he concluded, 'I can't draw it. Because the sea has no borders.'[2]

The Timor Sea opens west into the Indian Ocean and east into the Arafura Sea, which adjoins the Pacific Ocean. It is roughly

450 kilometres wide and covers an area of about 615 000 square kilometres. It is a relatively tiny sea, stretching the short distance between Australia's northwest coastline and the southeastern tip of Indonesia. Over the past century, Australian mapmakers have seen little problem in drawing the lines that for the Rotenese fishermen have transformed their traditional fishing grounds into a minefield of risk and uncertainty. Drawing lines in the sea, to the fishermen, is ludicrous. Sadli Hudari Ardani, another Rotenese fisherman, holds up to the camera a map handed out in Pepela by Australian Fisheries some years before to illustrate the areas where fishing is and isn't permitted. 'For fishermen like us, this map is nothing but a picture,' he sighs. 'Because there are no signs. No signs at sea.'[3]

The Rotenese, along with other seafarers from the diversity of islands and fishing communities in eastern Indonesia, have been crossing these waters in small wooden boats for centuries. They sail and fish the reefs and islands of the Timor Sea in search of marine products to trade on the Asian market. Once, the northern coastline of Australia was regarded as the southernmost rim of their maritime world. But Australia's steady seaward expansion over the past century has changed all that. In 1979, the formal declaration of a 200 nautical mile fishing zone took Australia virtually to the doorstep of eastern Indonesia. Since that time, the Timor Sea has become the most fiercely guarded of any in Australia's vast maritime estate.

The Rotenese fishermen's refrain that there are no lines in the sea is more than a statement against invisible boundaries. It is a defence of their own sovereignty, a protest against the dispossession of waters they frequented long before Europeans discovered them and Australia claimed them. The sweeps of the pen that created these lines simultaneously erased their history in these waters. Based on a mythical premise that the sea was empty and that therefore no one would suffer the loss of it, the Rotenese were suddenly cast as 'invaders' and evicted.

As any reasonably aware Australian knows, invasion has a particular resonance in the Timor Sea. Long before asylum seekers started utilising this ancient island-hopping route as a gateway to Australia in the late twentieth century, these waters were both feared and cursed for their geographical proximity to the 'yellow hordes' lying so close on the horizon. Christina Stead evoked the idea of the yellow peril when she named it the 'Yellow Sea'.[4] It has become the nation's metaphorical back fence in popular consciousness, 'Australia's backside pointing at the Asians', to paraphrase Arthur Upfield.[5] The nation spent the final years of the twentieth century looking backwards over its shoulder. It was the fear of being caught unawares, from *behind*, that drove these waters into the frontline of national security concerns.

And yet, looked at from Australia's northwest shoreline, there is little to suggest that these waters are one of Australia's dark places. Here the light illuminates everything in spare patterns of bright colour — the red-gold earth, the blue-silver sea. In the dry season there are few clouds to cast shadows. When the sun sets, it is with a rapidity that never fails to awe me, having grown up with an east coast city skyline, where the sun is either melting up or down, not dragging the world around in circles as it does in the north-west. To watch it plunge into the sea is a jolt. The sky suddenly erupts into fiery shards of orange and purple, fragmenting the surface of the waters below. In the hot summer months, dramatic lightening storms flash across the seascape. It is possible, then, to recall the tempestuousness of its recent history.

Despite its incarnation in the twentieth century as a bulwark in the defence of nation, the Timor Sea was once a bridge rather than a barricade between its two opposing coasts. Early Europeans viewed it as a welcome crossing to escape Australia to the relative safety of the Dutch colony of Timor. Mary Bryant, for example, a convict in the First Fleet, together with her husband, two children and seven others stole a boat and sailed it all the way from Port Jackson via the Gulf of Carpentaria to Kupang across the Timor Sea. Their ordeal apparently inspired many would-be followers.

More famously, the two European navigators Matthew Flinders and Nicolas Baudin, while on their missions to trace the contour and shape of the Australian continent, likewise viewed the Timor Sea as an avenue of retreat from the inhospitable waters of the north to the Dutch port of Kupang. In 1801, the Frenchman Baudin's decision to steer his ships north to 'the anchorage everyone hankered after with so great an impatience' was greeted with relief by his sick and desperate crew. 'The news had such an effect upon some of the sick on board, that several of them found strength enough to come up on deck to make sure it was really true.'[6]

'How great was the contrast between the beauties of such a situation, and the sterile and monotonous neighbouring shores of northwest New Holland,' wrote François Péron, a naturalist aboard the *Géographe*, as it anchored at the entrance to Kupang Bay. These early impressions of Timor soon soured as disease and defection decimated the numbers of the French crew, although the experience didn't soften their return to Australia's northwest coast, a place of even greater tribulation for the sailors. But as they and their English counterparts made their crossings back and forth in these first years of the nineteenth century, they were travelling a well-worn thoroughfare between the two coastlines. Indonesian seafarers had been using it to visit Australia's shores for centuries.

Flinders stumbled upon the evidence of it as he sailed westwards from the Gulf of Carpentaria along Australia's northern coastline. 'Indications of some foreign people having visited this group were almost as numerous, and as widely extended as those left by the natives,' he wrote, citing the remnants of pottery, bamboo, palm leaves sewed with thread to make hats, 'and the remains of blue cotton trowsers'.[7] In February 1802, as the *Investigator* navigated a narrow path between the mainland and a smattering of high, offshore islands, they suddenly rounded on six 'vessels covered over like hulks', lying at anchor in a small bay surrounded by a scattering of canoes. The chief of the six crews was a small, elderly man called Pobassoo. A portrait painted by the *Investigator's* young artist, William Westall, depicts him as a serious and dignified figure, his head swathed in a Muslim turban headdress, his robe pulled about him.

Although Flinders and his men had often come across the traces of these people before, they had never encountered them in person. Flinders had originally thought they might be Chinese fishermen, but now, with the help of his Malay cook to translate, Flinders learnt otherwise from Pobassoo, and much more besides, in the following two days. These vessels were in fact part of a massive fleet of some 60 boats and 1000 men that had sailed from Makassar in the Celebes to northern Australia with the powerful northwest monsoon. They were now scattered westwards along the coast, and had come in search of trepang, the edible sea cucumber or bêche-de-mer, a highly prized trade item on the Chinese market. Before noon the next day another five boats arrived. Apprehension about the numbers of armed men milling in canoes around his ship did not lessen

Flinders' curiosity. 'My desire to learn everything about these people, and the strict look-out which it had been necessary to keep upon them, prevented me from attending to any other business during their stay.' The interest was reciprocated. From Flinders, Pobassoo learned about the existence of Port Jackson, of which he was ignorant, and made his own notes, 'writing from left to right', about the Europeans.[8]

Baudin had a similar encounter. On his second visit to the northwest coast, almost eighteen months after the first, a landing party discovered several prows anchored at bay at Cassini Island in April 1803. All but one of the boats sailed away on their approach. On coming closer, the Frenchmen discovered that the five crew aboard the remaining boat were Malay fishermen in Timorese dress. Later, Baudin sent out a new search party to the island. On reaching the coast, the French sailors soon found themselves surrounded by a fleet of two dozen such boats. Once they had made their peaceful intentions clear, they learned that the men were on an annual visit to the coast to fish for trepang. From this encounter Baudin surmised that the early Dutch discoverers of New Holland some two centuries before must have been led there from the Moluccas by Malay fishermen.[9]

It is not known for certain when the Macassan crews started visiting Australia but the relationship is clearly an old one.[10] Pobassoo told Flinders that this was his sixth or seventh visit in 20 years, and for at least 300 years the great Macassan fleets made an impressive sight in Australia's northern waters, sailing in groups sometimes carrying as many as 2000 men at any one time. They called the Kimberley coastline Kai Jawa or Kaju Jawa, a name originating from the term for the mangrove tree.[11] The northern Arnhem Land region they called Marege. Both these coastlines were rich in the trepang delicacy so favoured by the Chinese. It was the depletion of sources along the South China coast that had led the search further south, to the region the Chinese called *Nan-Hai*, the 'Southern Seas'.

Aboriginal cave paintings across the north, some of them dating back hundreds of years, tell the story of the Asian seafarers and their boats. Tamarind trees planted by the fishermen stand in campsites littered with archaeological remains. Northern Aboriginal languages still bear traces of Indonesian words. The stories of the solo expeditions of Rotenese fishermen have been overshadowed in the history books by the impressive size and romance of the Macassan fleets, but they are part of the same history, pursuing the same catch for the same market. 'Macassan' is in some ways a misleading term, for the fishermen who made up the crews of these fleets were in fact from many parts of eastern Indonesia, and often of the same origin as the smaller-scale fishermen who sailed in single wooden boats called *perahu*.

The Rotenese fishermen have a long history in the Timor Sea that overlaps and transcends that of the Macassan fleets. Their traces can also be found along the Kimberley coastline, in Aboriginal languages, songs and paintings and throughout the reefs and islands in the Timor Sea. Perhaps their omission in historical narrative is due in part to the burden they carry of not being quite 'past' enough. Unlike the Macassan crews, who disappeared from the Australian seascape at the beginning of the twentieth century and thus earned their place in the history books, the story of the small-boat fishermen of eastern Indonesia is still being played out in Australian waters, courts and prisons. History has a special bias against the present.

For those living along its rim, the Timor Sea was a centre-piece of social and cultural existence, a thoroughfare and a lifeblood. The Indigenous communities that flank its margins are bound by an old maritime relationship. Once it would even have been possible to argue for Australia's northwest coast as the final extremity of southeast Asia. Nowadays such an idea seems absurd. The lines of demarcation are too firmly drawn. But a tiny flicker of a connection is still being kept alive. Some years ago, a group of elders from the One Arm Point Aboriginal Com-munity, north of Broome on the Dampier Peninsula, propelled by the ancient memory of the small wooden boats appearing each year to work the reef beds of the Kimberley coast, went 'to see for themselves' the place these visitors had come from.[12]

What they encountered was a shock. The poverty was confronting. But for Irene Hunter and her brother Eric what struck them most was how much this world, so foreign in so many ways, resonated with their own. These were a sea-people, their lives regulated by moon cycles, winds and tides. 'They like us. On the coast.' Everyday conversations were dominated by the subject of fishing. Boys became men in the sea. To the Hunters, the Rotenese were 'very gentle, very educated' people, nothing like the crass intruders of their Australian stereotype. Eric came away determined to find a way to help the Rotenese establish the trochus hatcheries that they were developing in their own community.

The Bardi step toward reconciliation is an anomaly. Australia has sought to maintain as much distance as possible across its northern seas. I followed the Bardi route to Rote in 2001, and the length of time it took to make the journey seemed at the time a telling metaphor for just how segregated the region has become in modern times. Despite the short distance of a few hundred sea-miles between my

departure point and destination, it took two planes, a
longboat and at least two days of travel. The only visitors
taking the short cut in the other direction have been the
Rotenese fishermen under arrest and the handful of 'boat
people' picked up trying to run the gauntlet of border
patrols.

At the time that I went to Rote, it was a little-known
fact that for over two decades hundreds of fishermen from
eastern Indonesia had been taking up space in Australian
jails, sometimes for months or years at a time. It was their
stories, gathered mostly during hasty, secret recording
sessions in the prison in Broome, that compelled me to write
a film script. During the making of *Troubled Waters* we were
forbidden journalist visas by the Indonesian government, at
a time when all Australian journalists were treated with
suspicion, and when West Timor had become notoriously
aligned with the people-smuggling trade. Getting to Pepela
became another exercise in secrecy. It was soon apparent that
telling the fishermen's stories was not going to be easy. We
faced the same barriers of secrecy, fear and suspicion in the
making of *Troubled Waters* that governed maritime relations
in the Timor Sea.

Once in Pepela, however, the experience could not have
been more different. The fishermen were willing to entrust
their stories to an Australian public. They talked of the many
things that make up the world of a traditional Indonesian
fishermen, the boats, fishing, their families and bosses, the
land they cannot till and, of course, the sea. I learned, in
talking to them, that the lines in the sea are more than
policed coordinates on the map. They are the fault lines that
divide the sea between two cultures and two histories,
between fundamentally different ideas of maritime
sovereignty and ways of imagining seaspace. For the
fishermen of Rote, their eviction from their traditional

fishing grounds has been more than a process of physical exclusion and criminalisation. It has been an exercise in the eradication of their history in these waters, the story of which tells the lie of Australia's 'empty sea'.

THE TIMOR CONNECTION

The northwest coast of Australia

HUMAN CONTACT ACROSS the Timor Sea has a long and rich history. Sailors from Timor and Macassar and the Indigenous peoples of northern Australia were well acquainted with each other for at least 200 years prior to British colonisation of Australia. Indonesian fishermen were almost certainly the first people of a different culture and race to meet with the Aboriginal people of the north.[1] Vanessa Poelina tells a creation story of a warrior man, 'coming from overseas and bringing a special bush and . . . planting it all along the river and creating the billabongs and the waterholes'.[2] For Vanessa, the story shows the ancient connection between Timor and northwest Australia. Her own family is a continuation of this history. Her father left his birthplace of Alor in the southeast Indonesian archipelago in the beginning of the twentieth century to cross the Timor Sea in search of a living. His journey represents a contemporary chapter in the history of these crossings, but its beginnings are to be found in the trepang trade.

John Crawford, an early nineteenth-century English visitor to the bustling port town of Macassar, capital of southern Sulawesi and the centre for the trade of sea products on the Asian market, had little positive to say about this much-coveted Chinese treat, but his vivid description certainly warrants repeating: 'an unseemly looking substance, of a dirty brown colour, hard, rigid, scarcely possessing any power of locomotion, nor appearance of animation'.[3] There were at least 30 varieties for sale in the Macassar marketplace, ranging in price from five Spanish dollars per *picul* to at least fourteen times that. No one, according to Crawford, understood the complex process of sorting and valuing the trepang except the Chinese merchants. Shark fins were also among the lucrative products being shipped through to China, 'articles of luxury rather than of necessary food among a sensual people,' he wrote, 'who seek them under the imagination that they are powerful *tonics*.'

In the early days of the nineteenth century, trepang fisheries were found in every country and port from Sumatra to New Guinea. The most productive of these were undoubtedly those in the Aru Islands and the Gulf of Carpentaria and 'generally on all the north-west coast of New Holland'.[4] Far from being *terra nullius*, 'empty land', the northern coasts of Australia were part of an interconnected and thriving maritime network of trade and commerce that centred around Macassar, and trepang was just one of many exotic commodities that passed through the region destined for the kitchens of China and Europe. In 1856 Alfred Wallace described an emporium of fabulous foods and spices that had travelled from as far afield as New Guinea, Borneo and the Gulf of Carpentaria to the warehouses and market stalls of the port city.[5] Shop merchants plied rattans from Borneo, white sandalwood and beeswax from Timor, trepang from Arnhem Land, cajuti oil from Bouru, nutmeg and cloves from New Guinea, local coffee and rice, pearls, pearlshell and tortoiseshell from the archipelago and the islands of the Timor and Arafura Seas.

Macassan fleets set sail from Sulawesi in the summer months, a time of powerful monsoonal winds. The might of these is still regularly proven by the remains of shipwrecks and all manner of debris from the islands of the Indonesian archipelago that wash up regularly on the beaches of the Kimberley coast. They embarked principally for Arnhem Land, but the Macassans also visited the reefs and coastal waters of the Kimberley to dive for and harvest trepang. Their route took them from Macassar to Rote and then a day's journey across to Ashmore Reef. From there, they would pass through Seringapatam Reef, reaching Cassini Island a day later. Aboriginal people from Kalumburu in the far north still remember the stories from their parents and grandparents about the fleets that would come to set up their base camps nearby and then head out to Champagny and Camden Islands.[6] Or they would sail to Cape Bougainville, another half day's sail. Other boats from Ra'as near Madura were known to sail directly to Cape Leveque on the Dampier Peninsula north of Broome.

Once the large fleets reached Australian coastal waters they would break up into smaller groups of around three or four boats, taking off in different directions to work the coast. Land bases were chosen for good shelter, usually among mangroves, and their proximity to fresh water. The crews spent each day taking out the canoes they brought with them in search of trepang along the reef beds and shallow waters. The catch was then processed back at the campsite. It was a sophisticated operation. Large iron cauldrons were placed above stone hearths. The trepang was boiled and then dried in temporary smoke-houses. There are still quite a number of these stone hearths in existence. There are also tamarind trees that were planted by the Indonesians to supplement a frugal diet, as well as pottery fragments, shellfish remains and even lead musket balls and flints from flintlock rifles.[7]

Presumably the Indonesians were armed to defend themselves from attacks by the local Aborigines. Work in Marege and Kai Jawa could be dangerous. John Roe, a lieutenant stationed in the northwest, wrote a letter to his parents in 1818 describing the inhabitants of the region as hostile, 'occasioned by the presence of the Malays on their coast, whose treacherous and perfidious dealings with them, have rendered the Natives equally as bad'.[8] Robert Scholl, the government-resident of the northwest, noted that the fishermen who visited Camden Harbour to collect water were afraid of the local Aborigines, and reported that 'some of these Malays had been attacked last year, one of them killed and others wounded'.[9] Matthew Flinders and his men were strongly cautioned by the Macassans they encountered on the northern Australian coast to 'beware of the natives'. The Macassan captain Pobassoo told Flinders that he himself had been speared in the knee. Shortly before their meeting another of their crew had been slightly wounded.

It is unclear how serious or how regular these outbreaks of hostility were. It is likely that the Macassan visitors sometimes trespassed on important sites, or overstepped cultural taboos. But equally, Indonesian camps were often in close proximity to Aboriginal campsites, meaning the two groups often lived adjacent to one another. They must have coexisted amicably. It was in both sides' interests to maintain an atmosphere of cooperation, and right across the north of Australia a certain unwritten code of conduct appears to have operated most of the time in their relations with each other. The Yolngu people of Arnhem Land, for example, remember the Macassan period as one of great independence, a time of cooperation and trade, and the creation of new rituals and acquisition of valuable new knowledge about other worlds beyond their own.[10]

Aboriginal people also worked for the Macassans, receiving payment in kind for their labour, and they learned to speak the language of the crews they travelled with. According to George Windsor Earl, an early European visitor to the region, nearly every Indonesian sailing vessel carried two or three Aborigines from the Gulf of Carpentaria. This was common wherever Indonesians worked in Australian waters.[11] Sometimes their travels took them all the way back to Macassar, to see for themselves the places their visitors had come from. A party of prospectors travelling in eastern Arnhem Land related a chance encounter with an Aboriginal man who spoke a few words of English, and astounded them by relating his visit to Macassar and further afield, to Singapore.[12]

In 1824, the Dutch governor-general, on a visit to Macassar, described the Aborigines he saw there as 'very black, tall in stature, with curly hair, not frizzy like that of the Papuan peoples, long thin legs, thick lips and in general, are quite well built'.[13] The Aboriginal travellers would have encountered a motley town of merchants and seafarers from all over Asia and the trading world: Chinese; Malays from Johor, Pahang and Patani; Spanish, Dutch, English and Danish entrepreneurs, businessmen and sailors.[14] Some became stranded overseas. In 1876, there were said to be about seventeen Aborigines living in Macassar, mostly from the Port Essington region. As the sea-historian Frank Broeze once observed, these interactions illustrated that for the people living along its rim, the Timor Sea was not a barrier but 'a place of work and the maritime road to Macassan society — the first steps in modern times to connect Australians with the peoples and markets of Asia'.[15]

The British attempted for a time to gain a foothold in the trepang industry and capitalise on the lucrative links between eastern Indonesia and northern Australia. George Windsor Earl was one great enthusiast for such a project. In his book *Sailing Directions for the Arafura Sea*, he wrote that a northern British settlement would 'become the emporium of the Archipelago of the Arafura, while the inexhaustible banks along that coast will nourish a thriving trade with China'.[16] But these colonial visions were tainted by a history of disasters that plagued attempts to create British settlements in the north. In 1824, Fort Dundas was built on Melville Island. The 120 soldiers and convicts had to endure starvation, scurvy, dysentery; the heat, flies and huge mosquitoes that came in great black swarms every dawn and dusk to attack every bit of exposed skin, and the tiny invisible sandflies that were even worse; the barren soil where they could make nothing grow and disastrous relations with the local Aboriginal population. All this soon drove the newcomers to death, despair or madness. Within three years the fort was deserted.

Fort Wellington at Raffles Bay on the Cobourg Peninsula lasted an even shorter time. In its first year, 1827, the entire settlement population was struck down with fever and sickness. Malnourished and debilitated by disease, bored, miserable and hungry, and completely at a loss in the strange environment, the remaining 70 or so lasted only another year. In 1829, the last survivors were evacuated.[17]

A mere seven years after the Fort Wellington debacle, renewed calls for a white settlement in the north to facilitate trade with the Malay archipelago appeared in the press. To some contemporary observers, these colonial entrepreneurs must have seemed to have either optimism in spades or very short-term memories. An article in the *Perth Gazette* in 1836 promised that a British colony 'in that part of the world would be attended with a fate as prosperous as that which marked the unparalleled success and advancement as Singapore'.[18] Unstated, but no less of a real concern, was that the French or the Dutch might get there first.

In 1838, Fort Essington was established to great fanfare and grandiose imaginings of a future rich in trepang and trade. Two years later, malaria struck, and in the intervening years between 1840 and the fort's eventual abandonment in 1849, the commandant, John Macarthur, reported that at times practically all of his men were crippled with fever. The place stank with sickness, decay and death. A visiting ship's surgeon in 1848 described the place in no uncertain terms as 'fit for neither man nor beast' that deserved 'all the abuse that has ever been heaped upon it'.[19] Those who could escape did. The rest were evacuated and with them went any real hope of making trepanging a British industry. Intermittent attempts over the next 50 years to harness the Macassan trade came to nothing. The Europeans had neither the knowledge, the skills nor the trust of the local tribes to make the scheme work.

The great Macassan fleets began to disappear from the northern Australian seascape after the 1880s. Their successful trading relationship with the local Aborigines must have irked the colonial authorities no end. The imposition of licences on the Macassans in the Northern Territory was one reason for their declining presence, but it is probably safe to say that the Macassans themselves started venturing elsewhere in their search for trepang. Certainly their disappearance from the Kimberley coast cannot be traced only to Australian licensing regulations, as no West Australian authority ever attempted to enforce licensing laws in places so far away from Perth in those days. In 1906, authorities stopped issuing licences to the Macassans altogether, and the following year, they didn't reappear.

For a long time overshadowed by their mighty Macassan counterparts, seafarers from the islands of Timor and Sulawesi continued to make their solo journeys via the reefs and islands of the Timor Sea to the Australian coast. They also came in search of marine products to trade on the Chinese market. Their connection to this time-worn sea route in all likelihood predated the Macassans, and remained unbroken after, and despite, the eviction of the Macassans in 1907.[20] Memories still linger among the Bardi people of the Dampier Peninsula of the foreign fishermen working the reefs around Sunday Island. Irene Hunter from One Arm Point Aboriginal Community, on the tip of the Dampier Peninsula north of Broome, recalled stories she was told as a young girl about the sight of Indonesian boats 'just one, maybe two kilometres off the mainland here' and 'a lot of Indonesians . . . just walking around on the reef just picking up the shell'.[21] Irene refers to trochus shell, which the Bardi people traded with white missionaries for food. Her own grandparents remembered Indonesians and Aboriginal people 'actually on the same reef at one time, shelling'. She also recalled seeing Indonesian fishermen from a distance in her own lifetime.

Pearling became the first real European fishery in northern Australia, taking hold with incredible rapidity on the Kimberley coast. The arrival of the Europeans to the pearl trade was predated by a long tradition of pearlshell harvesting among the coastal Aboriginal tribes of northern Australia, who lived alongside some of the richest pearling grounds in the world. Pearlshell could be picked up on beaches, along reefs exposed at low tide, in rock pools and rock crevices. The Bardi, Nyul Nyul, Jabirrjabir, Ngumbal and Yawuru tribes were engaged for centuries in collecting pearlshell to use for jewellery and as items of trade with the desert peoples. Ancient pathways carried the beautiful shell throughout the dusty interior of the continent and, later, seawards as well. Indonesian fishermen exchanged tobacco, rice and axes for it. Later still, the Europeans exchanged flour. In 1866, unemployed pastoralist William Tays and his Bavarian friend Seubert, camping on the Condon Banks near the De Grey River, gave local Aborigines three bags of flour in return for 9 tonnes of large shell. News of their find spread and hundreds followed, eager to capitalise on the desire for pearls sweeping across much of Europe. Pearling towns soon sprang up at Nickol Bay, Shark Bay and Cossack along the remote northwest coastline.

Like the goldfields of the 1850s, pearling attracted a transient, frontier population of hard-edged men, ex-convicts, ex-miners, ex-whalers, the young and the restless. Like gold, pearls offered the chance of instant wealth for the common man. 'There are two points in the adventure of the diver,' wrote Robert Browning in his poem 'Para celsus': 'One when, a beggar, he prepares to plunge, One when, a prince, he rises with his pearl.' One American scholar predicted in his doctoral thesis that 'whatever country in the wide circuit of the whole world was cursed with an abundance of pearl-producing oysters, would be sure, when the fact was discovered, to become a theatre for displaying the rapacity of the rest of mankind'.[22]

That rapacity was already in evidence in northwest Australia. In a practice that became known as 'blackbirding', Aboriginal men and women were kidnapped by pearlers and put to work. The shore beds were quickly exhausted, and Aboriginal slaves were forced to dive in deeper and deeper waters, young children and women, some of whom were in the later stages of pregnancy among them. Divers had their hands crushed by white masters when they clung to the sides of the boat, unable to go on, or were dumped miles from home if too sick to work. Sharks attacked them and exhaustion drowned them.

As pearlers began to encroach into deeper seas and the shoreline became a distant mark, the suffering of Aboriginal divers intensified. Forced to dive 6 to 8 fathoms repeatedly, blood would pour out of their noses and ears as they rose to the surface. At night their moans could be heard on deck, their bodies crippled with pain. Deaths were frequent. The infamy of the industry eventually spread all the way to Perth. One journalist expressed his disgust in an article for the *Inquirer* in 1875: 'The thirst for shells, for pearls, for success, brutalises . . . no day is respected, no dark man's life is valued . . . but the utmost of diving must be sucked out of them, killing them or not.'[23]

Public outcry eventually forced the passage of legislation that sought to protect Aborigines from the most flagrant abuses in the industry, but laws passed thousands of kilometres away were impossible to enforce on boats operating along a distant and remote coastline. While many disdained the new laws, other entrepreneurs turned to the old Timor Sea connection to find an alternative labour source.

The first Indonesians to work in the pearling industry were recruited directly from the islands of Alor and Solor, near Timor, in 1870. They were known as Malays, from what was then known as the Malay Archipelago (later becoming part of present-day Indonesia). Edwin Streeter with his partner Thomas Haynes recruited 61 divers from Solor, but 16 of them died in the space of a month. Still, according to Streeter, 'after their ears [eardrums] were broken, the Sooloo men did fairly well'.[24] In the space of a year, rough estimates

recorded a dramatic increase in the number of Malay
indentured labourers in the industry, from 225 in 1874, to
989 in 1875. But growing public knowledge of the abuse, the
non-payment and non-repatriation of the workers and the
staggering mortality rate eventually forced the Dutch
governor-general at Batavia (Indonesia being a Dutch colony
at this time) to introduce regulations to control the trade. The
use of Malays ground, temporarily, to a halt.

Aborigines, on the other hand, could still be exploited
for nothing. It wasn't until the shift further out to sea made
skin-diving impossible that Aboriginal labour was discarded.
The introduction of the hard hat and diving suit in the 1890s
catapulted pearling into a mass industry. Asians began to
replace Aborigines on the boats. The reasons are unclear, but
one argument is that Aborigines could not be persuaded to
put on a diving helmet to swim underwater. The racism of
the era also played a part. Cast as primitives, it was assumed
that Aboriginal people were incapable of using such technology. Some remained on the fringes working as shell-
cleaners, when they could get the work. Others, particularly
the women, were able to secure work as domestic servants.

Named a townsite in 1883, Broome quickly outgrew the
other pearling towns to become the main settlement along
the vast stretch of Kimberley coastline. The pearl rush shifted
north, emptying the earlier pearling towns of all but the
mounds of discarded shell, peeling tin and boat carcasses
rotting under the west coast sun. By 1901, Broome was one
of the principal and most lucrative pearling centres in the
world, a central player in the midst of a pearl mania gripping
the fashion houses of Europe. Luggers now went out to sea
for months at a time, and returned with mountains of
pearlshell. The industry became entirely dependent on Asian
indentured labour. Men from Singapore, Hong Kong, Japan,
China, Timor and the Malay Archipelago arrived at Broome

jetty by the boatload. Some were recruited in Singapore or Hong Kong by pearling agents such as Guthrie & Co. Seamen jumped ship in Darwin or Perth; still others made their way via the Timor Sea, all converging on this tiny Kimberley outpost to be assigned as crew on the hundreds of luggers punctuating the northwest seascape.

Broome's exotic population at the height of the nation's White Australia policy fascinated, puzzled and intrigued outsiders, entertained by stories of an oriental town of jumbled houses, opium dens, Japanese brothels and soup stalls, of pearls the size of dinner plates, of pearlers drinking French champagne out of tin cups and German beer in the afternoons. Broome's population was 'a microcosm of the universe', declared an article in the *West Australian* in 1910. 'Here are Eastern customs and Eastern clothes, Eastern life and — Eastern smells.'[25] Senator Staniforth Smith, visiting the town in 1902, described narrow crooked lanes that reminded him of Singapore, with 'flags, banners and strange legends floating from bazaars, houses, stalls and shops'.[26] He remarked that a visitor might be excused for thinking that a part of Asia had been detached and grafted onto the Australian continent. To visit the town meant that: 'Superficially, if not actually, one has left our very English Australia and has already crossed the small stretch of sea separating us from the rest of Asia . . .'

Broome may have been an anomaly in the context of its hinterland, but it shared much in common with the other port towns that stretched from East Asia around the Asian continent and across the Indian Ocean to East Africa.[27] These coastal cities were famously cosmopolitan and, like them, Broome's inhabitants gazed seaward to distant homelands and groups in other ports, and to the ships that came from trading ports across Asia carrying supplies in and pearlshell out. In 1901 there were 1358 people from Asian countries recorded in Broome, and 132 Europeans. By 1912, these numbers had reached 2309 and 274 respectively. The Japanese represented the greatest ethnic majority, earning Broome the nickname 'Jap Town' in its early years.

As the rest of the country threw itself behind the vision of a White Australia, Broome remained overtly non-conformist. For over a decade the white pearlers of Broome ran a tireless campaign to protect their use of indentured Asian labour. 'The industry will not pay white man's wages, and white men should not be asked to do the work,' stated one correspondent to the *Broome Chronicle*.[28] 'What we take is the harvest of the seas,' insisted another. 'It belongs to no one, as most of the fishing is done outside the territorial limits, and it does not matter to us what flag is afloat where our luggers are. '[29] Adept at finding ways to avoid the laws that applied on land, pearlers insisted that outside the 3 nautical mile limit, their business was entirely their own. Banjo Paterson's 1895 poem, 'The Pearl Diver', captured the attraction of the rich pearl-beds of the Dutch-controlled Indonesian archipelago for Australian and Japanese pearlers:

> Scarce grew the shell in the shallows, rarely a patch
>   could they touch;
> Always the take was so little, always the labour so much;
> Always they thought of the islands held by the
>   lumbering Dutch,
>
> Islands where shell was in plenty lying in passage
>   and bay,
> Islands where divers could gather hundreds of shell
>   in a day:
> But the lumbering Dutch, with their gunboats, hunted
>   the divers away.

> Joe Nagasaki, the 'tender', finding the profits grow small,
> Said, 'Let us go to the Islands, try for a number one haul!
> If we get caught, go to prison — let them take lugger and all!'[30]

Pearlers were already going to Kupang in Timor to recruit labour in the 1880s. In the 1890s, some started operating out of there using local Indonesian crew. The Dutch flag flying from their mastheads, these captains would return to the Australian coast, keeping just to the seaward side of the 3 nautical mile limit, and so were able to avoid the need for a licence. They avoided Customs duties on their supplies and pearl-shell, claiming exemption from both import and export duties on the grounds that they were 'foreign-going vessels working on the high seas'.[31] In this way they could restock with supplies on the Australian coast without incurring a fee or penalty. H. V. Howe, a Broome pearler during the pre-World War I heyday of the industry, related how in 1910 there were 25 vessels operating out of Kupang, six of them European-style schooners of 50 to 60 tons. The rest of the Kupang fleet was made up of traditional *perahu*, crewed and skippered by Indonesian sailors whose lifelong knowledge of these waters and their winds, tides, reefs and islands made them valuable assets to their Australian employers.

Henry Francis Hilliard was one such pearling captain who built up a thriving business in Kupang, becoming the principal agent for supplying Indonesian labour to the Australian pearl-ing industry. Hilliard built a strong fleet of Dutch-registered schooners and locally built *perahu*, which he also used to gain a foothold in the traditional Indonesian trade in marine products such as trepang, trochus shell and turtleshell.[32] His business success was largely due to his recognition of the enormous wealth of maritime knowledge and experience of the local seafarers around him, and his clever ability to harness the old sailing routes and fishing patterns that had been part of this world for centuries. His vessels would stop first at Rote to obtain supplies and then sail south to fish at the reefs in the Timor Sea. His name was known throughout the region, in Timor and in West Australia.

Henry's son Robin joined his father's operations some time around 1910, and in 1914 started his own business. Robin Hilliard learned his father's lessons well. Rotenese sailors first encountered him at Ashmore Reef on one of their seasonal fishing trips around 1918. Robin, upon meeting the fishermen, offered them the chance to work with him diving for pearls in Broome. The story goes that the fishermen couldn't say yes immediately, but had to return to Pepela to tell their families. Robin followed, and bidding their farewells they boarded Captain Robin's boat to Broome. Stories collected from the islands of Mantigola, Mola Selatan and Alor tell of similar recruitment of traditional fishermen by the enterprising junior Hilliard to fish the waters off the northwest coast of Australia. At the end of each seasonal expedition they would return to Kupang, where they were paid for their efforts.[33]

Indonesian sailors also came to Broome of their own accord. Georgina Kaissis was born in Broome to an Indonesian father and an Aboriginal mother. Her own father grew up on the island of Bau Bau, and travelled to the Tanimba Islands as a young man in search of work. While he was there he heard about the chance to work in Broome. Georgina told me that many made their way across the sea to Broome after they heard stories in the fishing villages of southeast Indonesian islands about the possibility of pearling jobs. When she was growing up, these men were known generically as Koepangers. 'Everyone called them [that], like Dad was Koepang, Uncle Sim was Koepang, Uncle Mudu was Koepang, they're all Koepang, when in actual fact they come from various places, Alor and Bau Bau and Flores.'[34]

Their journeys evoked the pre-European Timor connection with Australia's north. On board the boats the mariners developed a hybrid sea-language known as 'Malay talk' to overcome the language barriers between the various nationalities. Malay talk, or 'pearling-lugger pidgin', became the lingua franca of the Broome seascape, a nautical language combining Indonesian, Aboriginal Pidgin English — itself a product of the early pearling years — with some Japanese words thrown in. 'The Japanese people spoke Malay, the Aboriginal people spoke Malay, even white people spoke Malay,' Broome local Mick Manolis explained.[35] Pearling may have been a European enterprise, but the cultural world in which it operated resonated with a far older maritime connection.

Social relationships between Asian crews and Aboriginal women were strong in Broome. Another woman, born to an Indonesian father and Aboriginal mother, told me that the Indonesians were far more inclined to mix with the Aboriginal people in the town, and most of the Malay men had Aboriginal wives.[36] But these relationships were also illegal. Miscegenation was taboo. Fears that a new 'coloured' population would stain a White Australia were pervasive. Section 43 of the *Aborigines Protection Act (1905)* explicitly forbade social intercourse between Aborigines and non-Aborigines. But despite the vigilance of the authorities and Catholic missionaries in policing the two groups, Aboriginal women and Asian men actively sought each other out for company and the practice of cohabitation continued.

The *Broome Chronicle* in the 1900s was full of the trial notes of Asian men prosecuted for their contact with

Aboriginal women. Supplying liquor was a frequent charge. On 6 May 1911, for example, the paper reported that Tommy, a Japanese diver, was charged with 'supplying a native woman named Trilby with liquor. He made a statement regretting the offence and was fined £10, and 12s 6d. costs, or 6 months'. Tommy and Trilby were then charged with being drunk. The fact that this was Tommy's seventh offence and Trilby's third suggested something other than a problem with alcohol. Possibly they just liked to spend time together.

Some Asian men and Aboriginal women came together briefly, others established families. Under the *Aborigines Protection Act* of 1905, Aboriginal people had to get written permission to marry from the Chief Protector, an arduous, humiliating and usually unrewarding task. Some Aboriginal women who did attempt to go through the official channels were forcibly removed from Broome to missions for their trouble, while their husbands were evicted back to their countries of origin. Many others preferred to continue married life in secret, without the legal permission slip.

Relations were not only between the two sexes, as the official records might suggest. Asian and Aboriginal men also became friends. Vanessa Poelina spoke about a 'wonderful old man' called Uncle Dula, who used to spend a lot of his time with the local Aboriginal people. 'He fitted in quite well,' she laughed. 'He used to sit around in the corroborees and sing away with the Aboriginal people and the authorities of the time would come around and wouldn't suspect anything and he would just be there singing away.' Others spoke of the gambling that would go on all night, with all nationalities, excluding the Europeans, present.

The tiny town was segregated along racial boundaries. Georgina Kaissis explained that in the early years, the Koepangers lived 'up the hill. Further down around the corner you had the Chinese community and you had the Japanese

section in Chinatown which was about where the old jetty is.
The Malays lived down near the foreshore by the Conti
Hotel'. Stressful, overcrowded work and living conditions
sparked some famous riots between the Japanese and the
Koepanger/Malay camps, in 1914, and again in December
1920 and January 1921. The 1921 violence resulted in a
number of deaths.[37] As the years passed however, antagonisms
between ethnic groups died out. As Peter Matsumoto — a
man who describes himself as having 'little its and bits of
blood in me' because of his polyglot heritage — explained,
there were no more fights because 'you didn't know if you
were fighting your cousin or what!'[38]

⟶

Asian indentured labour remained a fixture of Broome
pearling up until the 1950s, but by this time the heyday of
the industry was long over. World War I had signalled the
beginning of the end as ships sailed off to Europe filled with
soldiers and arms, and the boxes of pearlshell stayed behind.
Buttons, the mainstay of the industry, were now being made of
wood and tin and the dealers in Europe shut their doors.[39] In
1918, the price for mother-of-pearl dropped to record low
levels, and the depressed market continued after the war.
The introduction of plastic dealt another crippling blow. The
Depression hit the industry hard, and in 1935 the destruction
of 21 luggers in a cyclone devastated the Broome fleet.

The Japanese began to leave. Those Japanese who remained during World War II were arrested and interned as
far away as Victoria and South Australia, often with their
Aboriginal wives and children. Peter Matsumoto and his
entire family (including his Aboriginal mother) were arrested
as enemy aliens and spent the war years interned in a camp in
South Australia. They were one of the very few families to

eventually return. As the Japanese disappeared, reliance on the Indonesian labour trade continued, and Kupang became an increasingly important centre for the recruitment of crews in the 1940s. But by this time, the Australian pearling industry resembled a shadow of its former glory.

The Timor connection was instead kept alive in the decades that followed by the families that had emerged out of the unique circumstances of the pearling industry, and by a far older maritime tradition. Fishermen from Timor and Sulawesi who had lost their pearling contracts returned to their seasonal fishing expeditions with the northwest monsoons. The pearling industry represents only one chapter in a far longer history of contact across these waters. For many Broome residents, these maritime links are as important as their Aboriginal identity. For Vanessa Poelina, her Broome family still has 'a strong connection with family in Rote ... Even after our father passed on we are still maintaining connection with family and the islands'. For these locals, Broome is still very much a 'part of Asia'. Its gaze remains fixed firmly seawards.

STAKING THE
TIMOR SEA

*Australia's history of
maritime expansion*

THE PEARLERS OF Broome may have looked across the sea with mercantile ambition, but for the rest of white Australia Asia's proximity was viewed as anything but advantageous for the new nation. 'From the far East and the far West alike we behold menaces and contagion,' declared Alfred Deakin in 1898.[1] Alongside the question of federation, a fervent fixation with the presence of a multitudinous Asia beyond Australia's shores dominated *fin-de-siècle* politics. Nor were these mutually exclusive concerns. Henry Parkes, five times premier of New South Wales between 1872 and 1891, campaigned for a new, united Australia bound by 'a crimson thread of kinship' to defend the continent against 'the countless millions of inferior members of the human family who are within easy reach of these shores'.

By 1901, fear of the diseased, alien, barbaric and over-populated Asiatic countries that crowded the oceanic edges of the tiny British outpost far outstripped any other strategic concerns of the population for the fledgling nation. The Chinese on the goldfields and in the towns and cities had already been severely dealt with. Laws preventing any further Chinese immigration had been passed in every colony by 1888. The seed of Asian invasion anxiety was sown in the earliest moments of Australian nationhood. The fearful gaze of a White Australia shifted seawards.

Australia started drawing lines in the sea virtually the moment there was a politically unified continent around which to draw them. The quarantine line was the first, a boundary 3 nautical miles out to sea that stretched around the entire periphery of the continent. Three nautical miles was based on the European 'cannon-shot rule', developed in the eighteenth century, the artillery range at which states could enforce their sovereignty. Called 'measures of defence at the frontier' at the time of its creation in 1908, it was a political but also a profoundly symbolic act, imagined as a 'very fine-meshed net' encircling the whole country.[2] It provided a sense of immunity and protection from the contagious populations hovering on the horizon. The first director-general of the Commonwealth Department of Health, John Howard Lidgett Cumpston, demanded the quarantine line be a call to arms: 'the seaward frontiers . . . must be fully manned and equipped with the most modern armamentaria in order that the possibility of invasion by disease shall be reduced to an absolute minimum'.[3]

The distinction between invasion by disease and actual invasion was, to his mind, purely academic, given that both threats came from the same source. It is all very well, he wrote in 1920, to have a White Australia, 'but it must be kept white. There must be immaculate cleanliness'.

The north posed a particularly serious risk. In 1911, the editor of the *West Australian* scoffed at the idea that disease could be stopped at the border. 'The stringency of our quarantine laws are unavailing as a means of protecting the north of the Commonwealth,' he wrote, 'while the unguarded coasts of the north offer easy access to all sorts of disease-laden Asiatics.'[4] Over half a century later, the West Australian Minister for the North West spoke of the dangers posed by the 'north being wide open to smuggling, the drug traffic, the introduction of disease risks and to illegal landings'.[5] And at the dawn of the twenty-first century, the fevered responses of politicians and civilians alike to the arrival of asylum seekers in boats in Australian waters saw a revival of the early associations of invasion and disease in the northern seas. In late 1999, Senator Ross Lightfoot, another West Australian politician, wrote to his local newspaper that 'if [refugees coming to this coastline] bring with them communicable, pandemic, epidemic or parasitic diseases (and they are from areas where contagious diseases are rampant), then innocent Australians could suffer'.[6]

The 'if' was rhetorical. Far from the centres of government and the civilising spaces of the towns, the north was seen as White Australia's curse. The sea may have provided the apartheid that nature had designed, but it was a precarious immunity.

Anxiety about the prospect of an Asian invasion gave the seas a special status in the politics of a newly federated Australia. The isolation they had once provided was no longer a guarantee against attack. 'It is more than likely, more than probable, that forms of aggression will appear in these seas which are entirely new,' mused Parkes. Naval defence was a key objective of Federation politics, and the focus of strategic policy in these early years was fixed firmly on the Asia-

Pacific. Any concerns about an external threat to the country's great tracts of 'empty' land from other European powers scrambling to take possession of the last unclaimed portions of the globe had largely dissipated.

Instead, it was Japan that was raising the alarm. Cut off from the rest of the world for centuries, Japan's sudden emergence from its self-imposed isolation onto the world stage was dramatic. News of Japan's decisive defeat of Russia's naval fleet in the Tsushima Straits in 1905 ricocheted across the Western world. Such aggression challenged not only Western imperial designs but racist stereotypes of Asian inferiority. 'Our deadliest enemy in the Far East is not Russia but Japan,' warned one English writer of the time, 'for she openly and avowedly sets herself out to be the England of the Orient. We do not require any Englands of the Orient.'[7]

In 1918, as the Great War drew to its bloody close, insecurity was peaking. The nation was but a tiny white drop in a coloured ocean, to paraphrase Prime Minister Billy Hughes. Sydney historian George Arnold Wood wrote dramatically: 'White Australia . . . is the watchword or warcry of a tiny garrison which holds the long frontier of the white world in front of the multitudinous and expansive peoples of Asia.'[8]

Watchword and warcry, fear and ambition — these twin impulses more than any other shaped the Australian strategic imagination in the twentieth century, and they were given their fullest incarnation in Australia's north, and in the seas that framed its coastlines. Hal Colbatch, the first minister for the West Australian Department of the North West, used these two driving forces of danger and opportunity to articulate the dream-nightmare the region represented in the national psyche:

> Its emptiness and its close proximity to teeming
> millions of coloured populations elevates to a position

of first-class importance the question of whether in the
years to come it shall be to the Empire an occasion of
anxiety and danger, or a source of boundless
opportunity and unlimited opportunity.[9]

In time, the region became all these things. Yet in the 1920s,
when Colbatch was writing his departmental booklet, his
constituency represented a remote but nasty thorn in the far
side of the continent for the visionaries of a White Australia.
Ever since New Year's Day in 1901, when Australia's inaugural
prime minister, Sir Edmond Barton, proudly declared 'a nation
for a continent and a continent for a nation', the question of
how to settle and protect the 'empty spaces' of the north had
become a national preoccupation, touted as one of the greatest
challenges that the island-nation faced. The vast absence of
white industry and settlement was seen as a dangerous entice-
ment to the Asian populations thought to be watching
greedily from nearby shores. Invasion, if it comes, prophesised
Parkes, 'will be stealthily . . . effecting a lodgement in some
thinly-peopled portion of the country'.[10]

A whole new genre of Yellow Peril literature was spawned,
finding expression through cartoons, short stories, plays, novels
and even films. Cartoons in the pages of journals such as *The
Bulletin* depicted hordes of diseased and barbaric Asiatics
bursting the seams of their own borders. Sydneysiders read
fictional stories by writers such as C. H Kirmess, in the Sydney
journal *The Lone Hand*, who used the theme of Asian invasion
to great dramatic effect. The 'alienated extreme Northern
corner — Australia irredenta — is flourishing with a hostile
population,' he wrote. '[The] Commonwealth must get ready
for its relentless march to the North to save the purity of the
race by sweeping the brown invaders back over the coral sea.'[11]

For some it was in the north that the success or defeat of
the 'great experiment of white Australia' depended. Peopling

the north was promoted by government as a patriotic duty, but this position had its detractors as well as supporters among the scientific elite. A huge debate raged in the first decades of the century over whether white people could live in the tropics. Those who opposed the idea believed that the very laws of nature precluded Europeans from surviving in a tropical climate, and that disease and racial degeneration would certainly follow such folly. As late as 1937 the geographer Griffith Taylor was still writing that the chief disability whites faced living in tropical conditions was 'tropical neurasthenia ... associated with depression, irritability, loss of mental activity, and power of concentration'.[12]

Taylor was sidelined by the prevailing orthodoxy, however. A younger group of scientists and medical experts linked to the Australian Institute of Tropical Medicine, created in 1909 with a clear brief to promote tropical settlement, argued that a healthy white population could not only exist in the tropics, but thrive. They forecast the development of a new British superman, a racial type especially suited to the exigencies of tropical living, 'based on British blood [who would] be British in sentiment, but would be amended by the sun and soil in appearance, physique, speech and temperament'.[13] The only problem whites faced in the tropics was the proximity of diseased 'coloured' people. If there was one prerequisite for the success of the ideal of a racially pure White Australia, it was 'the absence of any teeming native coloured population, riddled by endemic disease ...'[14] Eradicating disease, equated with Asians, was paramount to ensuring the survival of White Australia.

Australia's original 3 mile quarantine line was followed by a plethora of new boundaries over the next century. The nation's maritime expansion took place against the backdrop of new ways of imagining and legally defining the sea in the West. In the post-World War II era, the United Nations set about rapidly dismantling the notion of the 'freedom of the seas' that had governed the European world's oceans for centuries.

In 1789, William Blackstone had embodied the thinking of many of his fellow English jurists when he wrote that 'water is a moveable, wandering thing and must of necessity continue common by the law of nature'.[15] Blackstone believed the sea should be shared by virtue of its very nature, an ancient idea with roots in Roman philosophy. Classical scholars Virgil, Ovid, Cicero and Seneca all wrote of the common gift of the sea to mankind. Yet, despite its enormous romantic appeal nowadays, it is often forgotten that the legal development of the concept of the open seas was directly linked to the European ambitions of trade and empire.[16] Unfettered access to sea routes was crucial for ensuring imperial exploitation of the markets of the new world.

Hugo Grotius published his famous treatise on the principle of open seas, *Mare Liberum*, in 1604 on behalf of the Dutch East India Company with whom he was employed as a legal adviser. His concerns were first and foremost commercial. Grotius declared that the vastness of the world's oceans precluded the ability of nation-states to enforce maritime sovereignty, except over a narrow margin out from the coast. The idea of open seas was meant as a direct legal challenge to Spanish and Portuguese designs to divide the world's oceans for their exclusive navigational use. He decried the 'monstrous greed' of their intentions to leave only 'the narrow bounds of the northern seas' for the rest of the world.[17]

Thirty years later, John Selden came out with a treatise of his own in response to Grotius, *Mare Clausum*.[18] Selden was writing in support of Britain's attempts to exclude Dutch vessels from her waters, and argued that exclusive appropriation of inshore waters by states was imperative to ensuring the protection of maritime resources. Although Selden is often remembered as opposing Grotius, both advocated state sovereignty over coastal waters adjoining the land.

This transformation of coastal waters and shorelines into state territory entailed a complete overhaul of European fisheries. In medieval and feudal times, coastal and inshore fisheries were governed by a system of privilege, whereby feudal lords, often by way of kingly favour, exercised exclusive tenures in fishing grounds that were usually, although not always, attached to their lands. Privileges even extended to rights to particular types of fish. Under this system, the European poor had access to fishing grounds, as they did to land, by virtue of their social relationships to the privileged and an informal pattern of customary marine tenure that had evolved over time in small communities. Under the doctrine of the 'freedom of the seas', however, radical new rules of 'open access' governing coastal and inshore fisheries were instituted. Fisheries were absorbed by the state and became public property.

Opening fisheries up to *laissez-faire* capitalism meant that many local fishing communities lost the ability to regulate and determine access, the parameters of which had often evolved over long periods of time. Others refused to relinquish their customary marine tenure. The incursion of powerful commercial interests was resisted, sometimes violently, by fishermen across Europe and America. As one Massachusetts fisherman spoke out in 1871:

> Are the fishermen to be driven from their fishing grounds, are the people to be deprived of food, that a few men can be made rich out of the treasury of the sea? And has he or they only the right to catch fish who can afford the expensive and costly apparatus of the trappers?[19]

Although he was speaking over 130 years ago, his sentiments continue to be echoed around the world in fishing communities still fighting to retain control of traditional fisheries against the incursion of more powerful industrial interests.

The notion of the 'freedom of the seas' accompanied the appropriation of indigenous fisheries by Western colonial powers, often occurring as a footnote to the dispossession of adjoining lands. Western colonisers had little interest in or appreciation of the value of marine tenure. 'It not only ran counter to the tradition of freedom of the seas which they assumed to have a universal validity, but it also interfered with their desire to exploit the islands' marine resources — a right they tended to take for granted as soon as they planted their flags.'[20]

In 1992, the Australian High Court's landmark *Mabo* decision formally recognised Aboriginal sovereignty of the land prior to British invasion and paved the way for Aboriginal land rights. But recognition of the appropriation of Indigenous fishing grounds in Australia is dragging. On 18 September 2001, the first native sea title claim, known as the *Croker Island Seas* case, reached a conclusion in the High Court. Five out of seven of the judges ruled that the Croker Islander peoples do have native title rights in 3300 square kilometres of sea.[21] Unlike the *Mabo* judgment, however, these rights were not made exclusive. The right of the general public to continue to fish and navigate in these waters was not diminished by the finding. Instead, it gave the Aboriginal claimants the same rights to a limited resource as recreational fishers or 'user groups', rather than a responsibility as traditional owners to protect their waters. 'What they did was give us an empty plate without the fish on it,' a Gurig man said.[22]

Although the *Croker Island* case signalled a limited acknowledgment of Aboriginal sea rights at the top echelons of the Australian legal system, there is no such recognition of the customary marine tenure of indigenous Indonesian fishing communities in Australia's offshore waters. The connection the Rotenese fishermen have to the waters they call their 'gardens in the ocean' is virtually unknown and unrecognised in Australia. Their traditional claims are unlikely to ever exercise the same kind of moral poignancy, let alone reach an Australian court.

—

By the 1960s, the notion of the 'high seas' had given way to new ideas about maritime ownership and sovereignty. Recognition of the enormous wealth that lay under the oceans' surface drove this shift, precipitating massive sea grabs across the globe. Australia, the only continent in the world occupied by a single state, and by far the largest area in the world without a land border, benefited hugely from these changes. One of the largest maritime areas in the world came into Australian possession, measuring nearly 15 million square kilometres of ocean, practically double the size of its land mass.

The concept of the Exclusive Economic Zone (EEZ) is now one of the major pillars of the Law of the Sea. As the name suggests, the EEZ grants a coastal state exclusive rights to exploit its seas (to a distance of 200 nautical miles). In 1979, Australia declared its Australian Fishing Zone (AFZ) at the maximum distance, and in 1994 this was formally superseded by a fully operational EEZ around all Australian territories. This act of maritime expansion took Australia virtually to the doorstep of Indonesia. The AFZ sits just 80 kilometres off the island of Rote. Indonesia, an archipelago, also has its own EEZ, but as an archipelago the point of origin is taken at the island of Sumba.

The seas between Australia and Indonesia have been criss-crossed with more lines than any other maritime area in Australia's jurisdiction. Boundary negotiations have been

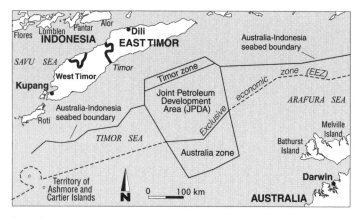

Maritime boundary arrangements between Australia
and Indonesia

arduous and protracted. It wasn't until 1997 that seabed and
water-column boundaries were finalised between the two
states, just two years before East Timor gained independence
and the rights to its own EEZ.

Along with the EEZ a huge raft of complex new
maritime laws, zones and principles was created, allocating
extra areas of tens of thousands of kilometres of seaspace to
states. The impact on indigenous fisheries was devastating.
Worldwide, the appropriation of traditional fishing grounds
suddenly turned local fishermen into trespassers and thrust
their communities into a cycle of poverty that few have been
able to escape. Now more than ever, as the world's fisheries
become more depleted and therefore more precious, low-
level wars, mostly fought out between small-scale, artisanal,
traditional fishing groups and industrialised nations are
intensifying. Rotenese fishermen are regularly arrested inside
the AFZ. They are but one example of thousands of other
fishing communities across the developing world which have
lost their right of access to their traditional fishing grounds.

A major development in international maritime law, and of critical relevance to the Timor Sea, is the concept of the continental shelf. In 1969, the *North Sea Continental Shelf* cases heard at the International Court of Jurisdiction set up at The Hague to deal with international maritime disputes, cemented the continental shelf principle in law. What the court said, in effect, was that a continental shelf running under the sea was 'an extension of the land mass of a coastal nation', and therefore maritime boundaries could be delineated from where they ended, up to 350 nautical miles from land. This gave Australia an extra 4.6 million square kilometres of sea mass, because Australia's continental shelf in the Timor Sea extends well beyond the 200 nautical mile limit. For Australia, it has meant billions of dollars in oil and gas reserves. But for the people of East Timor, it meant over three decades of war and impoverishment.

The section of the continental shelf at the heart of an ongoing dispute involving East Timor, Indonesia and Australia is called the Timor Trough. The trough runs pretty much parallel to East Timor at a distance of about 40 to 60 nautical miles offshore. In 1972, Australia and Indonesia negotiated a seabed agreement, during which Australia pushed hard for control of the entire trough, citing the continental shelf principle. Indonesia fought for a line of equidistance between the two countries, but the Australian position eventually won out. The Australian delegation celebrated its diplomatic coup with much fanfare, gaining control over 85 per cent of the area under negotiation. Professor Mochtar, leader of the Indonesian delegation, arrived back in Jakarta to condemnation for having 'sold the farm'.[23] Even so, things weren't completely resolved. A gap was left in the boundary line, a momentary break next to the island of East Timor and right at the source of lucrative fossil fuel deposits. It became known, infamously, as the Timor Gap.

In 1972, East Timor was still under Portuguese jurisdiction. Three years later, in the process of decolonising its
overseas territories, Portugal left. As the last of the Portuguese
officials departed, Indonesia invaded. Portugal's urgent
diplomatic warnings that foresaw a bloodbath in Timor went
unheeded. Australia stood back.[24] What followed was indeed
the bloodbath that Portugal had predicted. Australia's course
of action was already predetermined by the type of 'practical
hard-headed assessment of our real long-term interests' being
advocated by the then Australian ambassador to Indonesia,
Richard Woolcott. Australia's long-term interests were the oil
and gas in the Timor Gap. Closing the present gap in the
agreed sea border, he wrote, 'could be much more readily
negotiated with Indonesia than with Portugal or independent
Portuguese Timor'.[25] Successive Australian governments followed Woolcott's advice, sacrificing principle for pragmatism
in the pursuit of Timor's black gold. Their agenda was clear:
to close the Gap according to the continental shelf principle.
But Jakarta refused to do it, even despite Australia's explicit
recognition of its 'integration' of East Timor in the face of
worldwide condemnation.

In 1989, with no real resolution in sight, the two governments initiated an interim plan to create a 'joint development
zone' (JDZ) in the Gap. The agreement divided the 60 000
square kilometre area into three zones, one administered by
Australia, another by Indonesia and the third, the Zone of
Cooperation or Zone A, by a joint authority. Jakarta gave up
on its demands for a median line boundary to be drawn
between the two nations. In return, it got concrete approval
by Canberra for Indonesia's annexation of East Timor. The
image of foreign ministers Gareth Evans and Ali Alatas flying
over East Timor in a jet specially chartered for the occasion,
toasting each other with champagne and congratulating
themselves on being able to overcome their differences for

mutual benefit, flashed across Australia's TV screens. In the minds of many it represented the photo-snap image of Australia's recent history of moral and political bankruptcy in relation to East Timor. It came hard on the heels of the execution of over 5000 East Timorese people and fifteen years of a bloody occupation in which many more were jailed or exiled. Indonesia got East Timor, but ultimately Australia got the lion's share of the Gap's resources. For example, of the estimated gas reserves of 9.5 trillion cubic feet of the Greater Sunrise Field, 20 per cent lie in the Zone of Cooperation, with 80 per cent lying in the Australian area.

In 1999, after years of resistance against the Indonesian occupation, East Timorese independence became a political certainty. As the passing gunshots of the Indonesian military faded, the new East Timorese leadership was already working out how to secure the rights to the oil and gas fields off their coastline, the only real potential source of revenue that would enable them to rebuild their country. In the eyes of the East Timorese, the Timor Gap Treaty was an illegal document, and one for which they had already paid the ultimate price. As a new nation, East Timor was now free to claim its own EEZ. More importantly, the old continental shelf rule had fallen out of favour since the formal ratification of the United Nations Convention on the Law of the Sea (UNCLOS) in 1994. International maritime law now advocated a simple median line boundary between two coasts. Theoretically, under international law, East Timor was now entitled to all of the reserves in the Timor Trough. The East Timorese leadership legitimately demanded a radical redrawing of the maritime map.

This would have granted Dili exclusive rights over the petroleum fields previously shared in Zone A between Jakarta and Canberra, a massive loss to Australia of its lucrative investment stakes. There were also fears that Indonesia might retaliate by querying the legitimacy of the original 1972 border treaty with Australia, and demand its own renegotiated boundary according to the principle of equidistance. In the end, Australia, under the leadership of the Howard Government, refused to accede to East Timor's request for a new boundary line in the Timor Sea. Instead it offered East Timor a 20:80 split of future revenues from the Zone of Cooperation. By June 2001, responding to pressure, the offer increased to a 10:90 split in East Timor's favour.

On paper it looked reasonable. East Timor was set to receive $7 billion dollars over the next twenty years. Newspapers quoted the prime minister defending the 'fair deal' for Timor.[26] But in reality, by refusing to give up on the continental shelf boundary, Australia still controlled 80 per cent of an area where much bigger reserves and potential profits exist. East Timor would only get 90 per cent of the remaining 20 per cent (or 18 per cent of royalties) from the area, despite the fact that many believed East Timor was entitled to the lot. It meant a loss of a critical $36 billion for the struggling nation. But East Timor was in no position to argue with its powerful neighbour. On 28 June 2001, the East Timor government swallowed its pride and signed off on Australia's interim agreement.

The oil executives were still worried. It was common knowledge in business and government circles that if it came to the test, Australia's claims to the continental shelf boundary and thus to the Gap's oil and gas reserves would not be upheld at The Hague. In an astonishing move nine months later, and only one month before the new Gap Treaty was to be signed, Australia pulled out of the International Court of Jurisdiction altogether. A week earlier, East Timorese parliamentarians had attended a Timor Sea Petroleum seminar, at which they learned of their legitimate seabed entitlements under international law. 'Australia's strong view,' Foreign Minister Alexander Downer declared to the press, 'is that any maritime boundary is best settled by negotiation rather than litigation.'[27]

Two months later he went further, stating that while he was happy to hear what the East Timorese had to say, he 'would dismiss any proposals from newly independent East Timor to radically change seabed boundaries'.[28]

Any attempt by East Timor to get a legal resolution to the overlapping claims in the Timor Sea, let alone equitable maritime sovereignty, seemed sabotaged. The act was front page news in East Timor. Mari Alkatiri, East Timor's chief minister, described the move as 'an unfriendly act', but the East Timorese people were less reticent. On the first day of East Timor's formal independence, as John Howard and Mari Alkatiri signed documents inside, protestors raged outside the parliament building. Their banners read: 'Australia stop stealing Timor's oil.'

The dispute continues. In April 2004, East Timor and Australia again sat down at the negotiating table in Dili to discuss maritime boundaries. In his opening statement, Mari Alkatiri declared: 'For us, a twenty-year negotiation is not an option. Timor-Leste loses $1 million a day due to Australia's unlawful exploitation of resources in the disputed area. Timor-Leste cannot be deprived of its rights or territory because of a crime.'[29]

Australia is not alone among Western nations in pursuing a pragmatic and ultimately brutal agenda for oil at the expense of poorer nations. But these actions diminished any positives in the role Australia took in the political birth of the new East Timorese nation. No doubt for the East Timorese facing the terrible reality of years of debt and dependency, they were a stark reminder of their betrayal decades before.

—

'The sea of today is a used-up drudge, wrinkled and defaced by the churned-up wakes of brutal propellers, robbed of the enslaving charm of its vastness, stripped of its beauty, of its mystery and of its promise,' wrote Joseph Conrad at the end of the nineteenth century.[30] Conrad decried the destruction of the sea, 'an incomparably beautiful mistress, with inscrutable face, with cruel and promising eyes', by the onslaught of capitalism. In the more than 100 years since Conrad penned his despair, the seas and oceans, once regarded with awe for their subterranean mysteries, have become some of the world's most lucrative and contested territories, measured, mapped, appropriated, partitioned and raped of resources. 'The hand of the engineer tore down the veil of the terrible beauty in order that greedy and faithless landlubbers might pocket dividends,' he wrote.

In 2001, I stood looking out at the spectacular views of Darwin Harbour from the Northern Territory offices of Phillips Petroleum, a main player among the mining companies operating in the Timor Gap. I was interviewing the CEO, a large, jovial American, about his company's designs for the region. The installation of massive oil rigs was near completion, or perhaps already complete. 'What we are really doing,' he told me, 'is we're putting a city at sea.'[31] It didn't occur to him that he was building his city over another people's fields. After talking with him at length about the future of Timor Sea mining, there was no doubt in my own mind that Conrad was right. The sea of the past, untouched by the human hand of progress, is in ruins.

The oil rigs sit right on the periphery of the Indonesian fishermen's maritime world, like two towering sentinels on the horizon. They call them, in what seems almost Orwellian in its bluntness, Company One and Company Two. Their omnipotent presence is a powerful statement of ownership. Like watchtowers at the city gate, they seem to reinforce the fishermen's status as fringe dwellers, far removed from the big business end of the Timor Sea. Yet the fishermen know the contours and flows of these waters in ways to which the mapmakers, politicians and oil company executives are oblivious.

OF FISH AND MEN

The fishermen of Rote

SADLI HUDARI ARDANI has the lean, sinewy frame of a man who has spent decades on the open sea. Unusually tall, he is a towering figure in the Pepelan community, widely respected for his wisdom in matters historical and political, as well as maritime. He makes no attempt to romanticise his work. 'To be a fisherman, I feel this is not a contemptible job. But it's full of suffering. There is a lot more suffering than pleasure.'[1]

Traditional fishing is hard labour. Four to eight weeks is the average time spent on these voyages. A crew member must regularly pump the bilge water to keep the vessel afloat, as well as throw bucket water onto the decks to dampen them so the wood doesn't shrink. Rice and water, and whatever fish they catch for themselves, form the staple diet. A small cut-down iron drum is used to light fires for making rice and tea. 'In the heat all day and at night covered in dew.' The men sleep like sardines on the hard floor of the tiny hold, and the stench of dead fish can be overpowering.

Fishermen navigate by their knowledge of the winds, the currents, the skies, and certain landmarks. Stars are important markers of direction. The colour of the ocean indicates whether they are in deep or shallow water. Islands heat up at different times of the year and produce clouds that hang in the sky above, reflecting the turquoise of the shallow waters around them. They know when they are close to Ashmore Reef, because the light from the white of the sand is reflected in the clouds above in the shape of a banana leaf. Seas, weather and wind are unpredictable and can often turn nasty. 'Sometimes it's good, sometimes it's bad,' Sadli says philosophically. Without motors, radios, flares, life-jackets, or any of the other basic life-saving equipment Westerners have come to expect at sea, tragedy can be a hair's breadth away.

The fishermen of Pepela are unique in Rote. They have created a tiny world unto itself, based on a unique culture of sailing, fishing and trade sustained by the patchwork of reefs and islands in the Timor Sea. Pepelans commonly refer to these in poetry and song as their 'gardens in the ocean', or their fields. Another village on the northeast Rotenese coast, Oelaba, is also a traditional fishing community, and these two ports are the places of origin for the vast majority of the fishing boats, *perahu*, that journey down to Australian waters.

Elsewhere, the Rotenese are not open-sea fishermen, but they are, like the millions of other Indonesians living scattered throughout the archipelago, a coastal people. Seventy-five per cent of Indonesia's total area is sea, and over 41 million people depend directly on marine and coastal resources. In Rote, during the summer months when there is a break in harvesting the lontar palm, the mainstay of the Rotenese economy, the people regularly engage in fishing to supplement their frugal diet.[2] Their world is regulated by the rhythms of the tides, the ebb and flow monitored in monthly cycles that dictate the right times for catching fish that become stranded in the stone fish traps built along the shoreline. In the late afternoons people can be seen picking their way along the reefs and digging for shellfish at low tide. At night, thin beams of torchlight slice across the water.

No one in Rote lives out of sight of the sea. Its presence nourishes a parched and windswept interior of limestone and clay hills. The severe erosion of the landscape is caused by an aridity that rivals even the notoriously dry conditions of West Timor proper. Rainfall is about 1165 millimetres as compared with Timor's meagre 1500 millimetres. Rote is the poorest area in the Nusa Tengara region, alongside East Timor, and ranks as the poorest place in the entire archipelago that constitutes present-day Indonesia. The famous English naturalist Alfred Russell Wallace, travelling through eastern Indonesia in the nineteenth century, was amazed to see in the bleached, dusty landscape more parallels with northern Australia and New Guinea than southeast Asia. It was Wallace who argued for a dividing line, known as 'Wallace's line', through the Indonesian archipelago, from which the concept of an 'eastern Indonesia' evolved.

The Rotenese subsist on little. Besides fishing, gardening, wet rice cultivation and the herding of small livestock such as chickens and goats, the lontar palm is the centrepiece of their struggling economy. Considered one of the most efficient of the world's sugar-producing plants, it is an extremely valuable commodity on Rote Island. Cakes of crystallised sugar made from lontar palm juice are a major export to other parts of Indonesia. No part of the plant is allowed to go to waste. The leaves are used for thatching roofs, weaving baskets strong enough to carry produce to market and tight enough to hold

water, and for making sacks, saddlebags, mats, fans, traditional
hats, sandals and even cigarette papers. The fibrous leafstalks
are used to make ropes, bindings, straps, harnesses and bridles,
as well as fences and house partitions. In the early years of the
century the lontar's spiked leaves as well as the leaves of
another type of palm less common on Rote, the gewang,
were stripped to make sailcloth, which was regularly sold to
visiting sailors. In death the Rotenese are laid to rest in a
lontar coffin, and a lontar leaf knotted in a special way
becomes the symbol of the spirit of the dead person.[3]

There is a small palm grove in Pepela but Pepelans are
not, primarily, lontar farmers. Although I was dimly aware of
their culture as a sea-people, when I arrived in Pepela in 2001
I was unprepared for just how visual and explicit these connections are. The village is a celebration of boats and sailing.
The outside walls of the houses are painted in colourful
designs of boats and fishing scenes. Children sail hand-made
miniature *perahu* in the shallow waters. Young boys outdo
each other climbing to the tops of masts and jumping off
them into the bay. Men caulk the hulls of boats with
paperbark. Available ground between houses is laid out with
large striped canvas sheets being sewn into sails, on which
babies crawl, and children play around their parents at work.
Fishermen work together in a row to sandpaper long tree
trunks on the shore for masts. Along the foreshore women
collect the bits of wood washed up by the tide and bundle
them into firewood to sell for fishing trips. The open harbour
is a kaleidoscope of boats painted in bright colours. There are
no plain boats in Pepela.

The *perahu* has its own distinctive history in eastern
Indonesia. There are two main types of wooden sailing boats,

known as the *lete lete* (or sometimes *leti leti*) and the straight-keeled *lambo*. *Lete lete* are a type of long-distance trading boat used by the Madurese. These have a shallow, beamy hull with a short, pointed stem-post and a thick short mast set in the front wall of the deckhouse. The bamboo spars of the large lateen sail are fastened down to the foredeck. But Rotenese fishermen favour the *lambo*, the most recently evolved of sailing vessels in eastern Indonesia. These craft are essentially Western in design, in that they resemble the small trading sloop or cutter of the nineteenth century, and yet are traditional in their methods of construction.[4]

First the hull is formed with thick planks of hardwood that are shaped with an adze and joined at the edges by wooden dowels. Once the shell is formed, the ribs and floors are laid. Physically arduous, but also deeply symbolic, each step of the construction is accompanied by certain rituals that must be followed to ensure good luck and safety at sea. The way the keel of a *perahu* is built is one example of this. It is made up of three sections. The middle section is associated with productivity. It lies between the forward section, which represents the husband, and the aft section, which is the wife. Once the three parts are joined in union, the whole keel becomes female. The joining of the keel is a highly ceremonial procedure, whereby certain rituals are performed to simulate copulation, and even the order in which the keel sections are joined must conform to ideas about marriage and union between husband and wife.[5]

Once the construction of the *perahu* is complete, and this must occur in less than a year, the same time period as a pregnancy, a second ceremony is performed in which a hole is drilled in the keel. This ritual hole symbolises the *perahu's* navel, as it is the navel that is believed to be the point of attachment for a person's vital life force. A strong navel means good fortune. A coconut is wound eight times to the left and

nine times to the right around the boat to signify birth, a
ceremony identical to that held 40 days after the birth of a
child.[6] A coconut is then split in half over the boat. A goat is
killed and the head rubbed over the hull. Chickens are
sacrificed.

During my early visits to the Broome prison to talk to
the incarcerated Indonesian fishermen, I asked some of them
to describe their relationship to the sea. One of them, Rocky
Martinus from Rote, wrote a letter to me in response, in
which he described the ritual of launching a newly built
perahu on the open sea:

> First, before heading out to sea or out of the village, we
> have to feed the boat. This means, kill a rooster and
> spread its blood and flesh over the whole boat. Once
> I asked my elders why they did this. They said, once
> upon a time, there was a rooster crowing on a tree
> during the rainy season. It was a very strong wind. Hey
> friend, why do you shit on me and why do you sleep
> on me? asked the tree. Why? answered the rooster.
> Because if one day you will be used as a boat to go
> across the sea, then I will also be sacrificed, my flesh
> and blood.[7]

To describe the launch of a boat is also to describe the
beginning of a new personal relationship to the sea. Just as
young boys become men when they go out to sea, a *perahu*
that sails before having the chicken sacrificed is likened to a
woman who has not reached adulthood. When profit from
sailing is poor, the boat is compared with a woman who has
stopped menstruating.[8] And among the Bajo people, one of
the traditional seafaring peoples of eastern Indonesia, the
perahu is regarded like a child of its owner, with its own inner
life-force and spirit, and must search for a living just like a

person. The sea is regarded as the *perahu*'s mother. When the *perahu* is finally launched into the water, it represents the emergence of the baby from the womb.[9]

—

Fishermen time their voyaging by the seasons of the east and west monsoonal winds. The former starts in April, with strong easterly winds that usually last until July, followed by a period of lighter winds and then a period of calm, usually lasting between September and November. It is this period of calm that is considered the best fishing time in the Timor and Arafura Seas. In late November or early December, the west monsoon begins, bringing heavy rains, storms, squally winds and big seas, sometimes cyclones. This period lasts until March, when there is another period of light winds and calm until the next east monsoon.[10] It is risky to be at sea during the west monsoon or at the beginning of the east monsoon. Fishermen often talk about being forced to go fishing in the cyclone weather due to impoverished circumstances, but it is a dangerous time, as the little cemetery at Pepela attests. It has been estimated that more than 10 per cent of the male population of Pepela has died at sea in bad weather.[11] This number is likely to be much higher now. In 2004, 43 men died during one storm alone, a terrible loss for the tiny community.

Their dependence on its mercy demands that they demonstrate the utmost respect for the sea during the voyage. 'Because our relationship to the sea is very unique and has been for such a long time,' Yusuf Messak, another Rotenese fishermen wrote to me in a letter, 'it is our tradition that we are not allowed to make noise during the voyage, not allowed to hit the sea, not allowed to fight, because if we do these things, the caretaker of the sea will be angry and give us very bad luck.'[12]

Rocky Martinus also listed some of the rituals practised at sea to ensure good fortune:

> It is forbidden to dip the saucepan and the strainer in the sea because that way, you are inviting ferocious winds and waves. Do not throw leftover coffee straight into the sea. We must throw it on the deck. If we don't, during the night a ghost will appear and will change us and the boat as well. So if that happens, we must call each other different names and not our original names. If not we will die.

The traditional fishing community of Pepela is by no means ethnically homogenous. Home to a diverse concentration of peoples and languages, its polyglot character is the product of inter-island migration patterns, fluctuating trends in the world of maritime trade, economic pressures, and all the various 'broader processes of influence' which mould and pummel cultures into new shapes and forms.[13] The trend among traditional fishing populations to move around in search of new areas to exploit is nothing new. Maritime itinerancy has been recorded at least since the eighteenth century in eastern Indonesia, in an archipelago of islands and communities directly dependent on the sea. These 'swagmen of the sea' belong to a part of both Indonesian and Timor Sea history. As we have seen, at the beginning of the twentieth century the search for work took men as far as the northwest coast of Australia, and the history of pearling in Broome is intimately connected with these men and their journeys.

What has changed, however, is the demography of this development. Since World War II there has been a dramatic increase in the numbers of those who make up the population

of small-scale fishing crews in Oelaba and Pepela as people
have left other parts of eastern Indonesia, particularly Buton in
southeast Sulawesi, in search of work. The demise of eastern
Indonesia's own fisheries and reefs, in large part due to the
presence of foreign trawlers operating in Indonesian waters,
has exacerbated these numbers. Many of eastern Indonesia's
marine areas are in a dangerous state of near-collapse. Indonesian pelagic fishermen, who traditionally caught small
pelagics such as skipjack tuna and small mackerel, have
reported being driven to 'blast' fishing because foreign trawlers
moved into their areas in the 1980s. Blast fishing involves
using dynamite or crude home-made bombs. It is illegal, but
in the Moluccan Islands, for example, it is actively encouraged
by larger fishing companies who hire locals to do the work.
The live reef fish industry has also fallen prey to unsustainable
and dangerous methods, such as spraying potassium directly
onto the reefs to stun the fish.

Besides the native Rotenese, the islands of origin most
commonly named by the residents of Pepela include Sulawesi,
Binongko, Alor, Pantar, Flores and Java. Many have inter-
married with native Rotenese.[14] They tend to come from
five main ethnic groups, or *suku*: Makassarese, Buginese, Bajo
(also known as Bajau-Laut or Sama-Bajau), Butonese and
Madurese. These groups together make up a unique maritime
economy, based on their intimate knowledge of the sea, their
traditional navigating and boat-building skills and their fishing
expertise. They have collectively sustained an ongoing
connection to sailing, fishing and maritime trade. There are
hundreds of *suku* in Indonesia, but in eastern Indonesia, these
five are regarded as genuine maritime peoples.[15]

If there is any group that has retained some distinction, it
is the Bajo. Originally from the southern Philippines, the
Bajo began to migrate from the Sulu Archipelago as early as
the eleventh century, and are thought to have found their way

to Sulawesi sometime in the fifteenth century. During the eighteenth century they began to settle in the islands of Timor. They are known colloquially throughout southeast Asia as the sea gypsies or sea nomads, and their seamanship is legendary. They live their lives on, or in close vicinity to the sea, and they will often say they feel nauseous if they have to sleep on dry land or out of sight of the sea. One Bajo man on board a fishing boat in Pepela Harbour told me he had not been on land for many years. His face was etched with the deep lines that come from long-term exposure to the sun and wind on the open sea.

The Bajo are also renowned for their deeply spiritual relationship to the sea, for which they have seven names. It is medicine, home, a road, food, friend, brother or sister, and the home of the Umba Made Lau, their ancestral god.[16] They tend to work alongside or in close contact with some of the more powerful sailing peoples, the Bugis, Makasserese or Butonese, often supplying them with the catch to trade on the market through Makassar, which some still refer to as Ujung Pandang. After the collapse of the New Order government in 1999, the city reverted to its old name of Makassar.

But in some impoverished fishing villages where the Bajo settle, they face a tough time. Locals haven't always seen the romantic aspect to the Bajo presence. Their transient way of life means that they are often regarded as intruders and pariahs. There is a large Bajo population that lives in a segregated part of Pepela, along a narrow sandbank called Tanjung Pasir, separated from the main part of the village by a tidal creek and a low retaining wall, next to the local cemetery and near to the entrance to the harbour. Whereas Bajo had in the past used Pepela as a rest-stop to reprovision and wait for favourable winds on their way to fish in the Timor Sea, this changed in the late 1980s. Bajo fishermen began to migrate to Pepela and settle there. In 1994, Australian researcher Natasha

Stacey counted 42 houses on the Tanjung, of a total of 50 Bajo-occupied houses in the main part of Pepela. She recorded 292 people living in these houses.[17]

Rote is still a place untouched by the religious violence that tore other Indonesian islands apart in the late twentieth century. In Pepela, Muslims and Christians coexist peacefully side by side and crew boats together. Likewise the Bajo crew together with other Pepelans on fishing expeditions, but otherwise tend largely to keep to themselves. Although I didn't myself witness any overt hostility towards them from the other Pepelans, I am told that there are those in the village who look down upon the Bajo and regard them as less than equal members of society.

For over 500 years, exotic marine products dominated maritime trade relations in eastern Indonesia. Trochus shell, trepang, tortoiseshell, pearlshell and shark fin were all important trade items at different times. The intricate trade networks that developed between local sailing populations and the wider southeast Asian region, from Macassar to Singapore, was instrumental in enabling islands like Rote to escape the sort of aggressive colonial intervention that other parts of Indonesia endured. The Dutch occupied eastern Indonesia for almost 400 years, establishing the Dutch East India Company to colonise the lucrative sandalwood and spice trade in the region. But the Company was never able to gain any real control over the local maritime economy. Even as sandalwood and spices declined in Timor, the maritime trade flourished.

Trepang was enormously important right up until the twentieth century in shaping trade relations in the Timor Sea, and to this day is still collected on reefs in the old way, using the same shallow diving techniques of the Aboriginal skindivers of pearlshell over one hundred years ago, or of the Macassans even earlier. Men dive to depths of around to 12 to 15 metres, and sometimes as deep as 22 metres, with only a pair of wooden eye-goggles and sometimes a trepang spear. The catch is boiled, gutted and sun-dried, but instead of carrying out the process on land as was once done, it now occurs on board the *perahu*, which allows for a lot of weight loss in the catch and the opportunity to keep moving and catch more on one journey. The fact that Indonesian fishermen are no longer allowed to stop at Ashmore Reef, once a popular site for processing trepang, probably also has something to do with it.

The trochus shell is another major target of traditional fishing operations, and took over in significance in the latter half of the twentieth century. It has a pearly opalescent colour that makes it ideal for jewellery and ornaments, and an attractive substitute for mother-of-pearl. The depletion of the pearl beds in the early twentieth century shifted attention to trochus and this accelerated after World War II, when pearling went into further decline. Trochus is used to make necklaces, hairclips, bangles and rings. Less glamorously, it is used as a hardener in floor tiling, inlay work and varnish, and its nacre is utilised for the sheen in nail polish and in luxury car paints. BMW is one company known to use it.[18] Traditionally it was also collected for its meat throughout the Indonesian archipelago, Australia and the Pacific. Trochus fisheries in these regions account for about 90 per cent of the world's current supply, and in recent years shell prices have increased dramatically, a result of increased demand coupled with reduced supply. Stocks have been in serious decline for over ten years.

Since 1991, however, the major focus of Indonesian fishing operations has shifted to shark fin. Ardani is one of the two main boat owners and traders in Pepela, employing many of the fishermen in the village. In 1990, he switched from fishing for trochus and trepang to shark fishing because shark fin was where the profits now were. This trend is borne out by the much higher numbers of apprehensions by Australian authorities of boats engaged in shark-fishing in Australian waters. Favoured shark-fishing grounds include the banks of the Sahul and Holothuria and numerous Timor Sea shoals. The waters around Scott Reef and Browse Island are also popular locations. Traditional methods employed by the fishermen involve a 'shark rattle', basically a bamboo pole, at the bottom of which are a number of halved coconut shells stacked on top of each other. The fishermen stick it in the water from the deck of the boat, and 'rattle' it. The noise attracts the sharks, and baited handlines hook them in. Longlines, up to 250 metres or more in length, are common.

Agung is a young fisherman who was orphaned at an early age. He came to Pepela to find his maternal grand-mother when he was eleven. By the time he was fourteen years old he was the main support for his aunt, his two nieces and his grandmother, and had started crewing on fishing boats to provide an income. His uncle, Matteos Tungga, is a well-respected Rotenese fisherman who took him on his first fishing expeditions into the Timor Sea. Agung explained how fishermen catch shark. The first thing they have to do is catch small fish for bait, cutting each one into two pieces, one half per hook. 'Then we use the front sail of our boat to change the boat position. When the boat moves we throw our bait into the ocean.'[19]

This usually happens around five or six in the afternoon, and then they throw in the anchor and sit, waiting till morning to pull in the lines. 'If we catch shark we pull it into the boat'. Often it takes three or four of them, hauling in a line together hand over hand as they squat one behind the other along the prow. 'We cut off the shark fin from its back, tail and sides.' They dry the fin on the sides of the boat, creating a pungent smell of sun-drying flesh. It is, the fishermen say, not a hard smell to become accustomed to.

Gani Pello, who grew up in Pepela, sat with Agung as he related the process of shark catching. The more experienced of the two, he occasionally interjected with more detail. 'We don't let them totally dry,' he said at one point. 'We keep them under a canopy on the boat. We take them out when we are about to go back home. Then we dry them a little more. The reason we only half-dry them is so they will have more weight when we sell them.' I asked them about the wastage that occurred with this type of fishing, taking only the fin and leaving the rest of the animal. It is a common accusation levelled at the artisanal shark fishermen by Australian authorities. They were offended by this question. 'We don't cut off the shark's fins and then throw the shark back into the sea. We want the shark meat too,' Gani insisted.

They use a short machete to cut up the rest of the shark into small pieces. 'Some we bring home and some we use as our bait to catch other sharks,' Agung said. 'My family likes the taste of shark meat too,' Gani added. There are no doubt other fishermen who after hacking off tail and fins throw the body back into the sea, but the Pepelans I spoke to were adamant that they do not.

Prices and grades of shark fin vary according to the quality and quantity of their fin needles. White-finned sharks with the higher yield of fin needles, such as the white-spotted guitarfish, fetch the highest prices. The next most valuable are black-finned sharks, reef sharks, whaler sharks, then tiger sharks and hammerheads.[20] The fin needles contain elastin and collagen, and shark fin is a highly prized delicacy in many Asian countries, especially China and Taiwan, most commonly for use in shark-fin soup.

In Pepela there are four main traders, or middlemen, to whom the fishermen sell their catch. These men are called 'buyers', *pembeli*, by the fishermen, or more commonly *bos*, after the English word 'boss'. Each *bos* has his own networks and operates on a credit/debt system with the fishermen. They supply the provisions, capital, and often the boats to people who do not have their own. Natasha Stacey gives an account of two of the Pepelan traders, one of whom she calls *bos* 'A'. This man is the wealthier of the two, working for a husband-and-wife team from Hong Kong who provide him with capital to purchase sun-dried shark fin for export to Hong Kong. He owned, at the time of her research, eighteen *perahu* which he loaned to fishermen on credit. 'He works in conjunction with his uncle (*bos* 'B'),' she writes, 'who operates from his own premises and provides capital and provisions to fishermen on credit, with the arrangement that the fin is sold to *bos* A.'[21]

The way this works for the vast majority of traditional fishermen is that they are at the mercy of their boss, these days also the boat owner. 'We are just like fish-seeking robots,' said Sadli. The boat owner wants to make as much money out of his boat as possible. 'Even in bad weather they force a captain and crew to sail. We are forced to go, fishermen don't have any choice.'

Everything they need for a fishing expedition is bought on credit from the boat owner — in Pepela they call it *takan terangsu* — and this includes the food, sailing equipment and fishing gear. Any money that they make on the voyage must go first towards repaying their debts, and what little there is left over is split up between the crew. Unfortunately, the voyage itself is not the only cost that must be financed. Almost all the fishermen I interviewed in Pepela said that they also have to borrow money from the *bos* to give to their wives and families to use for food while they are away. This becomes an added debt they have to repay.

Gani explained that often the fishermen don't have good fortune on their journey, so the debts keep adding up, forcing

them to go out more and more often. The debt burden many
of the fishermen carry is astronomical. It affects every area of
their lives. They rarely if ever have the means to finance
fishing voyages on their own — I didn't meet anyone in this
category — and this translates into an ever-spiralling inability
to cover even basic household needs, education expenses for
their children (who often have to miss out on schooling
altogether), or medicine costs for sick relatives.

Even their houses are built on credit. Peter Isak Husein
built the little wooden house he lives in with his wife and
three children by borrowing a lot of money from his *bos*. The
house itself is one room with a palm roof and a dirt floor.
Every time he goes fishing he has to repay part of this debt to
the boat owner. It is, he says, 'a heavy burden'.[22]

A fisherman can never afford to fall ill. The biggest
tragedy for fishermen when they are held in overseas jails is
knowing that there is no one to support their families while
they are away, and that the best they can hope for is that their
wives, mothers or grandmothers have managed to borrow
even more to survive.

The fishermen all agree on one thing, that 'there are
no other jobs here. We don't have land to be farmers.
We don't have money to be traders. So the only thing we
can do is fish'.[23] In the 1990s, faced with mounting debts
and Australian pressure to cease traditional fishing practices, a number of traditional fishermen started to view
favourably the option of using their maritime skills to ferry
refugees to Australian waters. Sadli, burdened by over
3 million rupiah in debt, admitted to pondering this idea.
'I myself think that to carry some illegal migrants to
Australia would bring us a lot of money. But on the other
hand I don't think it is the right thing to do because that
could damage good relations between Indonesia and
Australia.'

It was 2001, at the height of the boat people 'crisis' in Australia, a time when the country was beset by anxiety over the issue of asylum seekers arriving on Australia's shores in wooden boats. I remember coming back to Australia after my Pepela journey and being struck by the vicious comments I was hearing on talkback radio. I couldn't help but compare the populist language of border protection with the careful reasoning of people like Sadli, living a hand-to-mouth existence yet who could still talk about taking a role in assisting good relations between the two countries. In light of the fact that the single largest external pressure Rotenese fishermen have faced in the past half-century is Australia's expansion of its sea boundaries in the 1970s, the contrast seemed especially stark. It was a humbling experience, to be in the presence of a man who had remained a true mariner, an honourable seaman in the face of such overwhelming odds.

MARE NULLIUS

The lines in the Timor Sea

IN 1949, A GOVERNMENT scientific research team on board the *Warreen*, a West Australian Fisheries research vessel, made a trip to Ashmore, Cartier, Scott and Seringapatam reefs to conduct a tuna survey. The researchers were startled by the unexpected scenes that awaited them in the middle of the ocean. At Seringapatam Reef they found 'Malay prows' with 'rattan sails, spars of bamboo and ropes of coconut palm' and several canoes attached.[1] Two days later, they arrived at Ashmore Reef to find 23 *perahu* at anchor. Fishing camps with wells of good fresh water, one of which was protected from pollution by a covering of stones, neat stacks of dried fish, drying racks, woven baskets, water-containers and bamboo poles resting in the sand demonstrated, beyond doubt, 'well established signs of occupancy' on the islets. The remains of

Lesser Frigate birds killed for eating were scattered about. The fishermen told the Australians they all came from Rote or Kupang. After spending two days at Ashmore Reef, the *Warreen* sailed on to Hibernia Reef, where they encountered another four *perahu* which 'made sail as we approached . . . Hailed one crew and were informed they were going to Roti'.[2]

All in all, the research team had sighted 30 *perahu* and around 300 fishermen at work. In an article he wrote about the discovery three years later, Dr Dominic Serventy, the senior scientist in charge of the mission, concluded that the fishing ventures he had witnessed were clearly nothing new. Indonesian fishermen clearly had a long history of contact with Ashmore and the surrounding reefs and were undoubtedly 'operating in some strength along the western portion of the Timor Sea, on islands and banks several of which are in Australian territorial waters'.[3]

His article appeared in 1952, the same year the *Pearl Fisheries Act* was passed in parliament. The Act made the collection of pearlshell, trochus, trepang and green snails to the edge of the continental shelf illegal, and marked the beginning of Australia's assertion of sovereignty outside the 3 mile nautical limit.[4] However, despite occasional sightings of Indonesian fishermen by lighthouse keepers or surveyors doing bouts of work on outlying reefs throughout the 1950s and 1960s there was little interest, and no action, taken. In the words of the West Australian Minister for Fisheries at the time, these were 'rather inaccessible waters', and the Indonesian fishing operations so 'well off the beaten track' there seemed little reason to apprehend them.[5]

In fact, for another twenty years the Timor Sea remained well outside the radar of Australian control. Knowledge of an Indonesian presence in these waters was sketchy and surveillance virtually non-existent. 'The WA Department of Fisheries and Fauna has four sea-going patrol vessels,' David

Brand, then premier of Western Australia, wrote to Prime Minister John Gorton in 1968. 'You may be assured they are available at all times for patrols of the fishing zone from Bunbury to Shark Bay.'[6] His statement revealed by omission the lack of attention to the Kimberley coast. The authorities of the day seemed quite content with an 'out of sight out of mind' approach to the Indonesian presence in Australia's northern waters.

Yet the 1970s heralded a sea change in Timor Sea affairs. The discovery of fossil fuel reserves lying untapped under the northwest continental shelf catapulted the neglected seascape into political consciousness. The shift in status of these waters, once 'inaccessible', now immensely lucrative, meant a whole new approach to the region and a sudden awareness of the substantial numbers of Indonesian fishermen in these waters. Australian officers sent out on surveillance flights and sea patrols were suddenly stumbling on Indonesian fishermen in their hundreds. Strangely, Australian authorities interpreted the strength of this presence as a new phenomenon, when in fact it was only Australia's discovery of the fishermen that was new. There was 'no problem off the WA coast about seven years ago' a Fisheries officer wrote in 1980. 'Till then the only known intruders had been the occasional apologetic fishing party swept off course by wind and currents.' Ten years later, the magazine of the Australian Fisheries Management Authority, *Australian Fisheries*, expanded on what had by then become conventional wisdom. 'Visits to the Australian coast stopped before World War I, with the exception of a few storm-blown arrivals.'[7]

The idea that intentional visits by Indonesian fishermen to Australian waters stopped before World War I, and that the only visitors thereafter were accidental and apologetic, was clearly erroneous, but it laid the foundation for the way history and policy would be written in these waters up until the present day. This is the myth of *mare nullius* — the maritime version of *terra nullius*, 'empty land' — the fiction that says that these seas were empty and unoccupied, that no one suffered the loss of them and that Australia's maritime occupation occurred without incident or harm. Like *terra nullius*, which assumed that the interior of the Australian continent was uninhabited but which was proven false early on in the course of white settlement, the idea of the empty ocean became a fiction of convenience, well before the process of maritime expansion was complete.

The historical connections between occupation of the land and sea are important. Australian authorities had little knowledge or experience of Indonesian activity in the Timor Sea. When evidence was presented to the contrary — and Dr Serventy's report of 1949 is one example of this — the theory that the ocean was 'empty' was, as Henry Reynolds wrote of *terra nullius*, a theory simply 'too convenient to surrender lightly'.[8] The authorities preferred to pursue the misconception that those fishermen they discovered had unintentionally strayed. This perception of a few wanderers accidentally blowing into Australian waters resonates strongly with the earlier image of Aboriginal people as itinerant and nomadic, and lacking in attachment to any specific region. The editor of the *Sydney Morning Herald* used this image to great effect in 1838 to justify European colonisation:

> . . . what is the difference between taking possession of a desert country without inhabitants, and taking possession of a country of which comparatively few wandering inhabitants make use? Such a country is desert for every purpose involved in this question, and may be justly occupied by civilized man.[9]

This concept of 'making use' was central to British notions of what constituted rightful ownership of the land. Like that of the traditional Indonesian fishermen 150 years later, Aboriginal people was classified as 'subsistence', a term that described, in the minds of the Europeans, a simplicity or primitiveness in method and approach to the land and a transient connection to territory. It was the opposite of farming, which implied an altogether more practical and sophisticated use of the land, and a relationship of longevity and permanency not apparent, so it was thought, in indigenous societies.

—

From about 1973, 'Indonesian fishermen had begun to intentionally find their way to the fertile WA waters. They now constituted a commercially oriented invasion'.[10] This remark, taken from an article written by a senior Fisheries officer in the *West Australian*, is revealing. In 1973, Australia started surveillance and policing operations in the Timor Sea. The date marked a new line in the sea, a temporal line that signified the moment traditional Indonesian fishermen crossed from being accidental visitors in empty seas to commercial invaders in 'fertile waters' in the Australian strategic imagination. The idea that they had suddenly forsaken a traditional subsistence lifestyle in favour of a commercial one was as flawed as the idea that their journeys into Australian territory were only newly deliberate. Indonesian fishermen have always been commercial operators, their fishing activities geared towards the collection of sea products for trade.

In 1968, the presence of Indonesian fishermen was identified in Australian legislation for the first time. Australia's unilateral declaration of a 12 nautical mile limit contained a direct reference to traditional fishing practices in the northern seas. It stated that Indonesian fishermen could continue to fish in Australian waters on condition that their operations were 'confined to a subsistence level', and only took place in a restricted area identified as those waters 'adjacent to the Ashmore and Cartier Islands, Seringapatam Reef, Scott Reef, Adele Island and Browse Island'.[11]

These were all favoured destinations for Indonesian fishermen, indicating an Australian awareness of their routes, but not of the fact that none of them were going there for subsistence purposes. Subsistence, which to the Australian way of thinking also meant traditional, was the opposite of commercial. In this vein, an Indonesian fisherman could not be traditional and commercial at the same time, although in reality this is what they all were. Six years later, a Memorandum of Understanding (MOU) signed between the governments of Australia and Indonesia repeated the misinformation and ill-wording contained in this earlier decision, and cemented it in law.

In September 1974, Australian Prime Minister Gough Whitlam and Indonesian President Suharto met in Jakarta. The rights of traditional Indonesian fishermen in the Timor Sea was one of the minor items up for discussion. The 1974 MOU, which developed out of these talks, was an agreement between the two parties that defined what, how and where traditional fishermen could access their old fishing grounds in the future. Still in place to this day, it was in all likelihood a hastily prepared arrangement, constructed during highly-charged talks primarily focused on the pressing issue of the future of East Timor. No Indonesian fisherman was ever consulted about the phrasing or design of the new arrangement. Worlds away from Jakarta and Canberra, the fishermen were oblivious to the creation of a document that would alter their way of life forever. When 'Operation Trochus' — a massive military sweep of the Timor Sea to evict the Indonesian fishermen from the area — was launched immediately following the implementation of the MOU agreement in 1975, they no doubt got the shock of their lives.

Effectively, the MOU did two things. Firstly, it created a designated area within which traditional Indonesian fishermen could fish, and secondly, it defined, for the purpose of legal access to this area, what constituted 'traditional'.

The designated new area outlined a 'box' within the Australian Fishing Zone. It stretches around five main reefs or islands in the Timor Sea: Ashmore, Cartier, Scott and Seringapatam Reefs and Browse Island. The largest of these, Ashmore Reef, is considered culturally and economically the most important to the fishermen, and is the closest to Rote, about 80 kilometres away. It has since been excluded from the original MOU terms, along with nearby Cartier. Adele Island, which was included in the precursory 1968 decision, and Rowley Shoals, which has been frequented since at least the nineteenth century, was never included in the 1974 MOU agreement, and so became out of bounds to the fishermen.

The outcome for the Rotenese fishermen was akin to the creation of a reservation at sea. It is an area that grows daily more barren as the pressures on its finite resources grow and the fishermen increasingly have to compete for the scraps.

If you examine the Box on a map, it has an angular shape, a bit like a square with one corner cut out of it and a knob at the top to include Ashmore Reef. This picture-frame approach is common in international maritime law. For the traditional Indonesian fishermen, however, the idea of carving up and boxing in sea-space, of creating lines in the sea, is a strange and alien idea. 'The sea is not divided,' Sadli exclaimed. 'They say we trespass the border. That's strange. How can we know we've trespassed the border? There are no signs. It's open sea!' Gani also tried to explain: 'If you look at the map you can see there's a border. But if you look at it as traditional fishermen we can't see it.'

Rotenese fishermen like Sadli work with the sea, Australian policy-makers work with two-dimensional paper maps of the sea. It is a different categorising of space, and the difference rests on interpretation of what constitutes knowledge. Compare these two images of another ocean, the Pacific. The first, a European map drawn shortly after the Portuguese explorer Ferdinand Magellan crossed it in the fifteenth century, shows it to be an empty expanse broken only by tiny fragments of land between the Americas and Guam until the islands of the Southeast Asian archipelago are reached. The second is the Tahitian's Oceania, a mental map of navigation created from knowledge of the skies, currents, winds and moods of the sea. This latter map differs because it is 'a sea of islands, not an empty expanse'.[12] Australian historian Greg Dening has also written of the intimate, complex knowledge of Oceania that came from what he terms a 'progressive series of encompassments'.[13] Bit by bit, over 2000 years, the Oceanians explored, voyaged, mentally mapped and signposted the 10 000 islands of this vast ocean, creating songlines and handing them down over successive generations.

Western maps, on the other hand, have historically been used as instruments of rule, to obliterate native boundaries and silence indigenous histories of place. Maps that followed the discovery of lands often served to legitimise colonial conquests. They made the world appear empty until cartographers inscribed the intricate lines and labels of European control.[14] These parchments may have been works of art, but their markings were often made without regard to the linguistic, ethnic, religious, tribal or any other social or political alignments already in existence. The Rotenese seascape, blanketed with centuries-old lessons of navigation and remembering, was erased by the new Australian map with its MOU Box.

Under the MOU agreement, the only fishermen who are permitted access to the Box are 'traditional fishermen', defined as 'fishermen who have traditionally taken fish and sedentary organisms in Australian waters by methods which have been the tradition over decades of time'. The important phrase in this convoluted and clumsy terminology is 'methods of use', which must refer to methods dating back at least twenty years, given the vague 'decades of time' reference. In other words, prior occupancy of the region has no weight whatsoever in this interpretation of who has the right to access these waters and who hasn't. Instead, the only fishermen who can claim to be legitimately traditional are those in sail- or paddle-powered wooden boats. Boats installed with small auxiliary motors, for example, are instantly classified as 'non-traditional'. 'You've got to look at the distinction between what is traditional and what is commercial, and anything that's got a motor in it, we'd say is a commercial venture,' an Australian Fisheries officer explained. What was left out of the equation is the unbroken history of Rotenese visitation in these waters.

One thing that struck me in my conversations with younger Rotenese fishermen is the way this concept of 'traditional' has been coopted to describe themselves. 'As traditional fishermen, we don't use motors. Sails are all we use,' they explain when discussing the nature of Rotenese fishing expeditions. They have learned to identify themselves, in the company of Australians, by using the rhetoric of Australian discourse. But these repeated conversations also reflect something else. The pervasiveness of MOU doctrine in the lives of these men cannot be overstated. Many have grown up in the shadow of the MOU and its laws. Their exclusive linking of the concept of 'traditional' with boat technology, without reference to the long-term attachment of Rotenese to these waters and their sense of belonging, implies an estrangement from their own history.

The absurdity of the MOU is that Indonesian fishermen are expected to stay within set boundaries, to exercise high-tech accuracy, without the technology that would allow them to do so. In its current wording, for example, radios and global positioning systems (GPS) would not be considered 'traditional'. Indonesian fishermen are often arrested for being a mere twenty kilometres or so outside the MOU boundaries. It's an irony not lost on some of the Fisheries officers who have worked on patrols around the MOU Box area. 'What the hell does a set of lines mean to an Indonesian fisherman?' one experienced hand asked bluntly. 'Nothing. I mean, all he's got is a rudimentary compass, he doesn't know what the latitude or longitude, north or south or east or west of this area is . . . it's very hard to say "Well gee, you know, your position is latitude 39 degrees and so south and so east" and they say "Oh yeah, that's good" — wouldn't have a clue.'[15] When Johni Fakie was arrested for trespassing and taken into custody, he couldn't understand the logic.[16] 'All we knew was the sea, mean the wide open sea. The sea had no signs that we had trespassed, and at sea there are no signs marking the border of Australian and Indonesian waters.'

Australian officers distinguish Indonesian fishing boats according to three different types. Type I is the sail-powered, double-ended, lateen-rigged vessel known as the *lete lete*. Type II refers to the *perahu* lambo favoured by Rotenese fishermen. These make up the vast majority of boats in Australian waters. Type III is a motorised boat. Unfortunately, these are arbitrary categories that don't make much sense in reality. Rotenese and Madurese *perahu* are often fitted out with small auxiliary motors. In the 1960s, an Indonesian government-sponsored program known as *perahu layar motor* sought to encourage traditional *perahu* craftsmen to install small motors for safety and efficiency reasons. In 1987, official statistics alone estimated some 111 000 *perahu* were fitted with small motors.[17] This means that what would otherwise be Type II boats become Type III when there is a motor attached.

The story of the arrest of the *Sirman Jaya* is typical of the way the legislation works in practice. Caught southeast of the MOU Box on Tuesday, 12 May 1998, the *perahu* was identified as a Type III motorised fishing vessel. In fact, the *Sirman Jaya* was a classic *perahu lambo*. The captain was a Bajo man from the tiny island of Maginti, just south of Rote. The equipment on board indicated that this was indeed a small-scale traditional operation. The arresting officer made a list of what he found on board: cane baskets, some bags of sugar for tea, two sets of goggles, plastic football boots, three handlines, one compass, a diesel motor and a drum of diesel fuel. The captain stated that he and his crew intended to fish for shark using the handlines and to collect trochus. The baskets were to store the trochus and the football boots were to be worn by the crew when walking over the reef areas where trochus is collected.[18] They weren't found outside the MOU boundaries. Nonetheless, the crew was arrested and put in detention, and the boat confiscated and destroyed.

Aligning the concept of traditional with primitive technology is hardly new to the MOU Box agreement. Western thinkers have been imagining indigenous societies in these terms for centuries. Right up until the mid-twentieth century, leading anthropologists perceived Australian Aborigines as a backward people who could never progress up the evolutionary ladder, their culture locked into a static and 'timeless present'. Western culture, on the other hand, was defined in terms of progress, and progress almost exclusively referred to technology. It was only in the 1980s that the Australian courts began to acknowledge the concept of cultural dynamism in relation to Indigenous people. In 1986, the Australian Law Reform Commission submitted a report on the subject of whether modern Aboriginal hunting and fishing activities could be considered traditional. 'Nylon fishing nets may have replaced those made of bush fibre . . . guns may very often have replaced spears, aluminium dinghies are used instead of dugouts . . . there was no reason that the incorporation of new materials should be considered as . . . not traditional.'[19]

In the 1992 *Mabo No. 2* case in the High Court, the judges recognised that the laws and customs of peoples do change over time and, more importantly, that this did not translate into a loss of traditional rights.[20] None of this has had any bearing on the Indonesian fishermen's situation. What makes these anomalies even more striking is Australia's approach to another set of foreign fishermen operating in Australian waters. The *Torres Strait Treaty 1978* between Australia and Papua New Guinea (PNG) regulates the activities of PNG fishermen within a protected zone in the Torres Strait. It defines 'traditional fishing' specifically in terms of the *purpose* of the activity, 'the taking, by traditional inhabitants for their own or their dependants' consumption, or for use in the course of other traditional activities, of the living resources of the sea . . .'[21] Commercial activities are excluded, because they are presumed outside the boundaries of a traditional economy. But what is interesting is that it makes no reference to the methods or technology PNG fishermen employ. Moreover, it recognises that customs can and do change over time. ' "Traditional",' the treaty states, 'shall be interpreted liberally and in light of prevailing custom.'

The sailing and navigational skills of the traditional Indonesian fishermen are legendary. Their ability to find their way in open seas without charts or other aids has consistently awed Western observers. 'Mate, I reckon they were bloody marvellous to be quite honest,' remarked one Fisheries Officer in the film *Troubled Waters*.[22] Their ability to sail for hundreds of miles and land 'smack dab' without any problems at their destination is a truly remarkable skill for those of us in the West who can't even contemplate a trip in the open sea without a GPS, compass, motor and radio, at the very least. 'I think they're natural seamen, I'd suggest that they could probably float a log around the world and still get there safely.' But this admiration for their seafaring skills has become something of a cliché, and for the fishermen a type of prison, in which they have become captives of a nostalgic, Western desire for the primitive.

There is, of course, logic in keeping Indonesian fishermen within a technological time-warp. They are less likely to inflict any real losses on what has belatedly become an Australian resource. This was stringently articulated by a Darwin magistrate in his decision to convict a Bajo captain from the island of Mola for illegal fishing in 1999. 'Clearly fish in the AFZ is an asset which the court jealously guards,' he stated, 'and an asset if not properly controlled will be plundered by people with no legal right.'[23] But underlying this is another impulse at work. In the same way that 'real' Aborigines are expected to throw boomerangs and live in tribes and humpies in the desert, 'traditional' fishermen are expected to keep going out to sea in little wooden sailing boats. To do otherwise, as those Aboriginal people who live in the cities have done, would be to forsake their right to the badge of Indigenous authenticity. 'The real secret of the primitive in this century has often been the same secret as always,' writes Marianna Torgovnick. '[The primitive] can be — has been, will be — whatever Euro-Americans want it to be. It tells us what we want it to tell us.'[24]

The exhibits of *perahu* in Australian museums also reflect this type of thinking. In Darwin, Fremantle and Broome, *perahu* have been donated by Australian Fisheries to local museums after their confiscations at sea, and turned into rare artefacts. A Pepelan boat, the *Sama Biasa*, was the first boat to be forfeited to an Australian museum, and is now on display in the WA Maritime Museum in Fremantle. The captain of the boat was Amin Pello, Gani's uncle. I am not sure what Amin would have made of his boat forever immobilised above sea-level, surrounded by the 'do not touch' signs. He would certainly have mourned the loss of a vital work tool. But to the uninformed spectator, the display is a quaint curiosity. 'To our eyes, it's an incredibly crude little boat for seven men to have lived and worked in,' reported the *Fremantle Gazette* of the museum's acquisition at the time.[25] 'However, closer inspection shows very careful workmanship in the vessel's construction . . . it's an example of the type of boat used by Indonesian fishermen for hundreds of years.' In reinventing the *perahu* as an apolitical piece of Australia's history, the Indonesian fishermen are also de-politicised. They, too, are turned into museum pieces. The article concludes: 'It was because this boat's crew were fishing for trochus shells for profit that their boat was confiscated and the men sent home.'

Amin Pello did find another boat after the confiscation of the *Sama Biasa*, but he died at sea only a few years later. His death, according to Gani, was a direct result of MOU regulations that keep the fishermen tied to outdated equipment and deny them the benefit of modern navigational aids. Many fishermen have drowned during storms at sea. Walking around Pepela, Gani points to the houses of friends that he has lost in this way.

'There are some very good friends of mine, they lived down there,' he says, pointing to a house halfway down a hill.[26] 'They were still young, nineteen and eighteen years old. Another friend, his house is here. This was my best friend Daed Hassan, he never returned.' Walking and pointing, Gani repeats the same story of death at sea. At one house, he pauses. 'This too is the house of a good friend of mine, Amrul,' he says. 'My boat was close to him when the storm hit.' It was a terrible storm, and struck in the middle of the night, so there was no way to see where his friend's boat was or if he was alright. 'It just disappeared like that. Till this very day, until this moment, we don't know . . . There were six people on that boat.'[27]

It's been estimated that in the ten years between 1990 and 2000, at least 140 fishermen from Pepela died while fishing legally in the MOU Box, and possibly many more.[28] In 1994, for example, 32 fishermen were lost at sea, during a particularly bad cyclone season. A newspaper report at the time acknowledged that fishermen 'had long wanted to use small engines to enable them to sail free of deadly cyclones which frequently hit their traditional fishing grounds'.[29] In one storm in 2004, 43 Indonesian fishermen died at sea, many of them from Pepela.

In 1998, a letter appeared in the *West Australian*, written by a group of fishermen incarcerated in Broome prison. 'We, the traditional fishermen of Papela, on the island of Roti, would like to tell our story', the letter began:

> Now we are allowed to fish only in a small area in the middle of our fishing grounds called the MOU. It is a poor fishing ground so we must fish for most of the year. Our sailing boats are not allowed to carry motors and because of this hundreds of our fishermen have drowned in the cyclone seasons. If the winds and

currents are unkind to us and we drift out of the
MOU we are arrested and towed into Broome.[30]

Perhaps the fishermen hoped that by telling their story to the
Australian people in this way, it would become apparent that
it was the law that was archaic, not, as it might have appeared,
their way of life. Sadli also approached an Australian Fisheries
officer who was on a visit to Pepela a few years ago with a
scheme that he believed would not only reduce accidents at
sea but also lessen border violations at the same time. He
suggested that the Rotenese *perahu* be fitted with engines, as
they had once been under the Indonesian *perahu layar motor*
scheme. Neither the letter nor Sadli's proposal got anywhere.
The presence of engines, Sadli was told, would only encourage greater violations of the MOU boundaries.

The MOU Box took effect on 1 February 1975. The
tragedy is that nearly 30 years, thousands of arrests and any
number of deaths later, the fishermen still can't see the lines in
the sea, and the line-makers still can't see the fishermen. The
imaginary lines that fence in this reservation at sea are not
only the sites of ongoing confrontation between Australian
law-enforcers and Indonesian fishermen, they are the political
boundaries of the struggle over history, maps and beliefs.

HOOKS AND SINKERS

Indonesian fishermen
and the Australian state

FOOTAGE SHOWN ON Australian television in the mid-1990s shows a Royal Australian Navy (RAN) vessel drawing alongside an Indonesian *perahu* in open seas. Through a microphone the naval officers command the crew to stop their boat. The frigate, measuring over 110 metres long, is powered by high-speed turbines and equipped with the latest in modern maritime technology including sonar, radar and torpedo systems. The *perahu* they are chasing, in comparison, is toy-sized. The wooden hull is exposed through the flaking paint. Its one sail is made of striped plastic. The crew squat on the deck. An officer turns to the camera and smiles: 'I love it when they try to get away.' Bullets are fired a short distance from the Indonesian boat. The clip ends with the fishermen waving frantically at the Australians.[1]

It wasn't always like this. Confiscation of any catch believed caught in illegal areas and a warning not to come back were the *modus operandi* of Fisheries officers aboard these patrols in the early years of the MOU Box. One Fisheries officer remembered the interactions with the 'old burglars', as he fondly recalled the Indonesian fishermen, as 'more a meeting of friendship . . . we had a pretty good relationship that went on for some time'.[2] He mentioned Sadli by name, saying that they often encountered the same fishermen at sea and were on familiar terms. 'We would go across in the motorised dinghy and it was fraught with all sorts of danger, with seas that were rough and boats turning over and all the rest of it, but we used to board them and greet them, see what they had on board, and if they were in the wrong seas we'd kick them out . . . and if they were doing the right thing we'd congratulate them on doing the right thing.'

During the 1990s, however, the culture of maritime compliance began to change. Fisheries officers were no longer always stationed on board the patrol boats. A roughness replaced the old familiarity of interactions at sea. 'One point is, the language barrier,' one fisherman said. 'It is a very confusing situation . . . because of the language barrier they thought we didn't follow their instructions and that made the [naval] officers angry.'[3] Officers started boarding Indonesian boats carrying guns, and some fishermen spoke of being pointed at with guns, handcuffed and manhandled.[4] One young man called Saryono was sick with malaria when the *perahu* he was in broke apart under tow. 'He was shaking,' the captain of Saryono's boat recounted. 'So this Navy man hit Saryono's head three times with a stick [baton].' According to the captain's story, Saryono vomited and passed out.[5]

I met Saryono in Broome soon after this incident. At the time he was one of a group of three fishermen brought out of the Broome prison on work release for a few hours each day, to repair a beautiful old *perahu* that had been donated to the Broome Historical Society museum by Australian authorities. The boat took up most the rear courtyard, at the back of which a demountable shed, known euphemistically as a donger, housed the museum's only microfiche. I was spending my days there in the welcome relief of air-conditioning, trawling through the Broome newspapers of the early 1900s. Outside, three Indonesians in green prison garb worked day after day to transform the flaking, broken wreck into its former seabound glory. Through the museum fence they could look out at the sea, broken up by the line of mangrove trees fringing the shoreline. They were the first Indonesian fishermen I had ever met. Despite the language barrier, they became my first teachers about the world they had come from.

Saryono was nineteen. He told me he came from Pepela, from a long line of seafarers. When I next saw him, it was years later in Pepela. He took me by surprise, suddenly coming up to me in the fringe Bajo settlement along the shore. Saryono, it transpired, was Bajo, and the man who greeted me was virtually unrecognisable from the subdued teenager I had met during those tea-breaks in the museum courtyard. On the beach in Pepela he told me how he had just got married. But a year after our reunion, like so many of the people in these villages, he caught tuberculosis and died, at the age of 25.

———

At the turn of the twenty-first century, new legislation increased the powers of military officers at sea. The *Border Protection (Validation and Enforcement Powers) Bill (2001)* granted the Australian Defence Force extra powers to pursue, board, search and detain vessels *outside* Australian territorial waters and detain people they only *suspected* of illegal activities. The new security laws were intended to allow RAN officers more powers to intercept boats of asylum seekers travelling via Indonesian ports. But as any fisherman knows, the wider the net is cast, the more little fish get swept up with the big fish (or vice versa, of course). In the years following the introduction of the Bill, record numbers of Indonesian fishermen have been apprehended by Australian authorities.

The militarisation of Australia's maritime territories is symptomatic of a fear of invasion that has plagued White Australia since its inception. Nowhere more so than at the sea border have these fears been so acutely imagined. The weaponry used to patrol the national fence is supposed to be a panacea for these fears, but their presence acts more to both incite and validate them. It becomes a circular exercise. If the weapons are there they must be needed. If they are needed, it must be serious. And so on.

Complaints by Indonesian fishermen of verbal or physical harassment at the hands of Australian personnel rarely, if ever, receive much credibility in the courts. The fishermen have only their word as evidence. Moreover, there is an unspoken official sanctioning of aggression at sea. Protecting borders is men's work.[6] Politeness has little place in the harsh world of border security, a world that operates far away from the civilising space of land, 'somewhere between our society and the societies of others'.[7] Keeping this world of aggressive border politics as remote and invisible as possible is necessary, not least because it represents such a contradiction to the values of the democratic, non-violent society it is set up to protect. A European fixation on internal security, freedom and prosperity has frequently led, para-doxically, to external savagery and violence. The history books are full of the stories of blood spilt, of massacres and dispossession, of bitter wars waged under the noble and cleansing banners of progress, civilisation and democracy.

Once a crew is apprehended at sea, they and their boats are towed to the north Australian coast, either to Darwin or to Broome. Often the boats don't survive the experience. The strength and speed of an Australian patrol vessel far surpasses that of the *perahu*. Towed long distances at speed, it is no surprise that they tend to break up under the strain. Fishermen will often stay on board their boat, pumping the bilges to keep the boat afloat, and even bailing if it starts to sink. Ultimately, however, those boats deemed unseaworthy are scuttled at sea.

Apprehended in 2000, Sadli described how his boat started to take on water during the tow, and the officers pumped more water into it to make it sink, 'but it didn't sink, it was still drifting. They were not satisfied yet. They then shot my boat with about three hundred bullets'. Sadli felt powerless. 'Realising that I was dealing with Navy people who have weapons and not from the same country as us, I knew there was nothing I could do. We were all crying at that time. And they clearly saw our tears.'[8] Sadli was later acquitted of any charges in an Australian court, his boat destroyed for nothing.

The first port of call for apprehended Indonesian fishermen is either the makeshift immigration detention centre on a private coastal property at Willie Creek, about 20 kilometres north of Broome, or Darwin Harbour. Willie Creek consists of a small bay at the mouth of the creek that becomes a sandbank as the massive Kimberley tides drop by up to 7 or 8 metres each day. Here the fishermen anchor their boats. From the beach there is a track winding up a small cliff that leads to the caretakers' property and a couple of makeshift sheds for emergency accommodation in the cyclone season. In Darwin, the facility for their detention is a designated

Quarantine mooring area about 200 to 300 metres from Stokes Hill Wharf, cordoned off by buoys. In both cases the fishermen are expected to camp on their boats until their court hearing. Those who arrive without a boat are usually billeted on other *perahu* already detained.

In Darwin it's a curious sight — the *perahu* bobbing away within clear view of local fishermen hanging their lines off the wharf's edge, the tourists with their cameras and the hundreds of diners who frequent the popular food stalls and restaurants along the jetty. The Indonesian detainees are visible yet completely isolated. They are only allowed off their boats once or, at most, twice a week for exercise, and even then under strict escort.

At Willie Creek there is no such visibility. The property is removed from the outside world. The only visitors tend to be the Fisheries officers who come to escort them to court. They have more freedom of movement, however, because they are not totally confined to their boats.

In a report released by the Federal Ombudsman's office in July 1998, the Ombudsman made specific mention of the fact that there were serious anomalies in detaining fishermen under the *Migration Act (1958)* until their court hearing. In the report, the Ombudsman stated that 'these people do not wish to migrate to Australia . . . but have been brought here, against their will'.[9] Further, detention, the report found, should 'not be prolonged or punitive in nature'. In 1997, for example, fishermen who pleaded guilty spent an average of 27 days in detention even before they went to prison. Those that plead not guilty wait longer. Conditions are cramped, with often seven or eight men forced to live together in boats that are rarely longer than 10 metres.

In the Ombudsman's opinion, the 'ongoing detention of the fishermen on their boats in Darwin or in the present facility at Willie Creek both involve unsatisfactory features, even for short stays'. Instead, the fishermen 'should be held in facilities of a reasonable standard appropriate to both the general length of detention and the particular circumstances of the fishermen'. Although over six years had passed at the time of writing since this report was released, no real changes have been made. When I asked why the fishermen were being kept in what were clearly substandard conditions, the Minister for Fisheries, Senator Ian McDonald, explained: 'They're certainly not boats or conditions that I or most Australians would want to live on, in fact under Australian law most of those boats wouldn't be permitted to operate in Australian conditions. [But] these are village people from Indonesia. They've already lived on the boat for a long period of time and they feel comfortable there.'[10] Primitive people, it seemed, were used to primitive conditions.

A report for *Insight* on SBS Television in August 2003 about the unexpected death of an Indonesian fisherman in Darwin Harbour, and a coronial inquest in Darwin in February 2004, brought to public attention the issue of neglect in the treatment of Indonesian fishermen in detention.[11] Mansur La Ibu was one of six fishermen on board the *Yamdena* when his boat was apprehended 52 nautical miles inside the AFZ, three days after it had departed Indonesia, on 28 January 2003. The *perahu* had a small diesel motor, but otherwise carried no other modern instruments or conveniences. The crew was arrested, and the *Yamdena* towed the 240 nautical miles to Darwin, where the men were detained on their boat in Darwin Harbour.

On 25 February 2003, the captain, Basri, woke up around 2.30 a.m. to see Mansur shaking uncontrollably. Cradling him in his arms, he alerted the other crew members. After two minutes Mansur stopped breathing. The other crew members tried desperately to shout for help, but it was a stormy night. They couldn't be heard by the two caretaker employees on the mother ship, anchored at the wharf. 'Because it was raining people couldn't hear us yelling', the police statement of Risman Wabulah, one of the *Yamdena* crew members, reads. 'We tried turning on the engine but it didn't work. We untied our boat off the mooring and drifted . . .'[12]

It was over an hour before assistance came. Mansur was transported to the pontoon area of Stokes Hill Wharf and an ambulance called. At 4 a.m. Mansur was pronounced dead. His body was taken to the Royal Darwin Hospital, and hospital records noted it was an 'unknown cause of death'.[13]

One of the issues canvassed during the television report was hunger on the boats. Fishermen on board the *Yamdena* alleged that Mansur had been hungry on the night that he died. Risman's statement reads, in part: 'We didn't have any lunch yesterday, we didn't have any tea . . . because we ate all our rice for breakfast.' Later, it says: 'Mansur swam from our boat last night about 11.30 p.m. to another boat to get something to eat because he was very hungry.' The *Yamdena* was one of thirteen boats detained in the harbour that night. 'When Mansur came back we all asked him what did he eat and he said he only ate rice because they ran out of food.'

Insight did not suggest that Mansur died of hunger, but the idea that detained fishermen went hungry was startling. One of the vice-consuls from the Indonesian Consulate stated that captains had made representations to him on numerous occasions to request additional food.[14] This was backed up by members of the Darwin Indonesian community and Indonesian fishermen, all of whom independently raised concerns about inadequate provisions of food to detained fishermen, as well as the lack of adequate sanitary facilities, inability to access help in an emergency, lack of proper exercise, and the length of their detention. The conditions of detention also prompted the Northern Territory coroner, Greg Cavenagh, to find that 'the standard of such detention in the case of the "Yamdena" for some weeks where their only shelter (and sleeping accommodation) is a small box . . . is unacceptable'.[15]

The Darwin marine charter company in question, Barefoot Marines, admitted in the Darwin Coroner's Court that the fishermen complained of hunger, but put it down to an attention-seeking exercise. They denied any accusations of neglect. As the Australian Fisheries Management Authority (AFMA) contracts out the care and management of Indonesian fishermen to private companies in Darwin and Willie Creek, it is ultimately their responsibility to provide for better facilities. The government is now moving to establish onshore detention facilities in Darwin for Indonesian fishermen awaiting court proceedings, or pending their repatriation. Coonawarra Detention Centre, an unused facility originally built to detain asylum seekers, is the most likely option. Whether this will do anything to alleviate the lengthy periods fishermen are spending in detention awaiting trial, and even whether it will mean better care, is debatable. It will certainly further entrench the status of most of these men as virtual prisoners, held without charge, without trial and without access to judicial review.

Mansur's body lay in the Darwin morgue for almost four months. His parents, from a remote village in the Aru Islands, were unable to pay for the cost of returning his body home. They only requested that he be buried as quickly as possible in accordance with Islamic law. Both the Immigration and Fisheries departments refused to pay for the cost of his burial. Eventually, an elderly Indonesian pensioner, Sujoko, heard about the body and raised the extra funds himself to bury Mansur. The local Moslem community buried him in an unmarked grave on 16 June 2003, at a ceremony presided over by the local Imam. Some months later, a married couple whose own young son was buried next to him bought

Mansur a headstone. The mother now tends Mansur's grave as well as her son's.

Mansur's parents were never consulted about the coronial inquest into their son's death, despite there being a lawyer appointed to represent them. Last year, Mansur's elderly father boarded a fishing boat. He was arrested, and during his detention in Darwin, after the intervention of the Indonesian consulate, was allowed to make one visit to his son's grave. Getting arrested was the only way Mansur's father could ever make this vital journey. Mansur's mother, in all likelihood, will never get that chance.

＿

When Indonesian fishermen appear before an Australian court, they are charged with using a boat for commercial purposes, and/or being in possession of a foreign boat equipped with nets, traps or other equipment for fishing without a licence in the AFZ. Trials are held in the Broome and Darwin Courts of Petty Sessions. Despite the fact that the fishermen are charged with offences under Commonwealth law, there have been discrepancies between the ways the fishermen are processed in the two states. In Darwin, lawyers from the Northern Territory Legal Aid Office still represent the fishermen in court. In Broome, they get no legal aid. Since 1989 in Broome, moreover, all crew members are charged with the offence. In Darwin the crew members are usually let off with a warning on their first arrest and only the captain is charged. Mansur was never charged.

Until recently, first-time offenders in Broome were placed on a good behaviour bond of between $10 000 and $14 000 for a period of four to five years, their vessels forfeited unless they could afford the extra bond for the boat, their catch confiscated, and the fishermen flown to Denpasar.

Nowadays the maximum fine for a first offence is $27 000. On their second fishing offence, or if they are found in breach of the terms of their good behaviour bond by showing up in the AFZ within the bond period, they are given fines ranging in severity according to the number of times the defendant has been arrested and the nature of the conviction. These penalties become *de facto* prison sentences because no one is able to raise what are clearly exorbitant amounts for a traditional Indonesian fisherman. They leave the court in a paddy wagon to serve out their fines at the rate of, at last estimate, $100 a day.

One magistrate of the Broome Court defended the current system of fines. 'We cannot say, "Well the dollar in Indonesia is useless, or people have nothing there so therefore we're going to (fine them) 20 rupiah", no, that wouldn't work.'[16] Handing down the fines as prison sentences has simply become a ritual of the court. No one — fishermen, lawyers or magistrates — seriously believes these will get paid. The Broome magistrate omitted to mention the fines when talking about sentencing in an interview for the film *Troubled Waters* in 2001. 'If they come back a second time,' he said, 'I may give them between six months and nine months' imprisonment term. If they come back a third or fourth time, they might get a little bit more, so twelve months, fifteen months.' The captain, he added, often cops a bit more.

La Bau Wajo was among the three fishermen whom I befriended along with Saryono at the Broome Museum. He had extensive experience of the Australian courts. La Bau came from Maginti, a tiny island — one kilometre long and 400 metres wide — southeast of Rote. Many Bajo fishermen live on Maginti and La Bau himself was a Bajo man. When I met him in 1995, he was serving a prison sentence of 220 days. Previously, he had spent 200 days in jail in 1990 and again in 1991. After his repatriation to Indonesia on the occasion that I met him, he was caught illegally fishing in February of the following year and convicted to another ten months in jail. In 1997, only three months after his release, he was arrested again on a fishing trip and given another twelve-month sentence. In 2000, he was sentenced to 400 days.

At the age of 31, La Bau had already spent almost a quarter of his life in Australian prisons. He was clearly an extreme case, but his story of repeated incarceration is not that unusual. Aside from the obvious question of whether lengthy prison terms actually deter Indonesian fishermen from breaking Australia's laws — and the evidence clearly suggests otherwise — their imprisonment contravenes two important legal principles. Australia is a signatory to the United Nations Convention on the Law of the Sea, Article 73 of which states that it is forbidden to impose a penalty that includes imprisonment for offences committed in the Exclusive Economic Zone, except where there is an agreement to the contrary with the other states concerned.[17] There is no agreement to the contrary with Indonesia and no provision between the two countries for the incarceration of Indonesian nationals found guilty of fishing illegally in the AFZ. Article 73 has been incorporated into Commonwealth legislation and therefore *should* now have the force of domestic law in Australia.[18]

Australian magistrates continue to circumvent these international obligations. In Western Australia especially, courts have justified the harshest prison terms available by relying on the WA Sentencing Act and, more specifically, a legal precedent created in the landmark 1991 case in the WA Supreme Court, *La Ode Arifin and Others v. Colin William Ostle and Others*. His Honour Justice Pidgeon stated two things in that case. He acknowledged that imposing a fine beyond the defendant's means, and without time to pay, was contrary to proper sentencing principle. However, he also decided that ultimately, where the only option is a fine, 'it must reflect the gravity of the offence and must be imposed even though it is known that the defendant will serve a default term by reason of his not being permitted in the jurisdiction in order to pay the fine by other means'.[19] Pidgeon's decision has become rule of thumb in sentencing Indonesian fishermen. 'My only option is to impose a fine. If I impose a fine, it must reflect the seriousness of the offence,' a Broome magistrate said when handing down his sentence in 1998. 'If I were to fine you on your level of income it would not be a deterrent.'[20]

It is the position of the Australian courts, in the words of this same magistrate, that 'subsistence lives are far outweighed by the seriousness of the offence'. His comment reveals a startling myopia. One fisherman spoke of his despair outside the Broome court after having a ten-month sentence imposed. 'This magistrate doesn't know what it is like, he has never ever been poor. He locks up the breadwinners and crucifies our families.'[21]

The extraordinary cost, in human and financial terms, of pursuing a punitive strategy of *de facto* incarceration for fishermen whose motivation to offend comes from a situation of poverty is difficult to comprehend. A far less costly and more sensible option would be to assist the fishermen to develop alternative sources of income in their communities. Although there have been some attempts by the Australian Agency for International Development (AusAID) to explore ideas for delivering aid to poor fishing villages, Pepela has, for the most part, been left out. Recently a new project was being investigated to help establish seaweed farming on some parts of Rote, but this is still in the research development stage. Instead, aid projects have targeted fishermen from areas not dependent on the MOU Box or Australian waters. There was once an attempt to give funding to buy a *perahu* in

Pepela, the fishing proceeds of which were then supposed to be distributed in the community. The *perahu*, however, was apprehended in Australian waters, taken to Darwin and destroyed.[22]

—

Confrontations at sea between Navy frigates and *perahu* are revisited in the courtroom. Indonesian fishermen, often barefoot and poorly clothed, face a forbidding array of Australian officers from the Navy, Fisheries and the state. Jill Elliott, a prison officer in Broome during the 1980s and 1990s at the time, attended a number of these trials. She was struck by the picture of inequity that they presented. 'It was the might of the establishment against poor uneducated fishermen and . . . it just didn't make sense,' she said. 'They put everything up against them, money, resources, lawyers. It was heartbreaking.'[23]

Aside from money and resources, the fishermen are handicapped by the language barrier in the courtroom. The presence of an interpreter is not always of much benefit. One of the interpreters who was used in Broome for a time spoke Malay, not Bahasa Indonesian. Another, an Australian man who is still to my knowledge used extensively in court proceedings in both Darwin and Broome, speaks passable Bahasa, but most fishermen from eastern Indonesian have Bahasa as a second, third or even fourth language. They speak the Austronesian languages which are linguistically distinct and separate. The Butonese, for example, who make up one of the dominant sailing populations of eastern Indonesia, speak at least fourteen different languages.[24] 'I didn't really understand him, because he spoke too fast in Indonesian, and he used high Indonesian language — you know, the official one,' one Indonesian prisoner told me after his trial. 'And we only finished primary school, we don't use that kind of language he's using in the court.'[25]

But the communication barrier is as much cultural as it is linguistic. La Bau, already an old hand at these trials, articulated his feeling of disenfranchisement with the legal process when he addressed the magistrate. 'It would not matter what I said to you, you will not listen to me and you will not understand.'[26]

Johni, at eighteen, was a newcomer to the Australian court process. 'I stated to the judge that actually we didn't consider ourselves to be guilty, although we had been accused . . . because the boat we sailed on was not a modern boat but a traditional one.'[27] In addition, he told the judge, his mother relied on him as the eldest in the house. 'Because my father died in 1990, I had to take over my father's job as a fisherman to earn a living and provide for my younger brothers and sisters and my mother.' He was hoping for the judge's sympathy, he said, so they might be sent home with their boat. But in the view of the court, the evidence against him was incontrovertible. He had trespassed a precise boundary line. Johni's idea of justice, on the other hand, was altogether different to the rational principles of Australian law. He believed that if he could convince the judge to feel compassion for him, at a basic human level, this would override a guilty verdict. His defence failed. 'Perhaps they don't have much sympathy for their fellow human beings,' he concluded. 'We're humans too.'

It is extremely rare for Indonesian fishermen to win their case should they decide to fight it. Pleading not guilty often means spending an extra period in detention before the case can be heard, and this can be anywhere from six to twenty weeks. This extra time in detention is not counted towards the length of their prison term, making it, in effect, an extra penalty. Most, when faced with this prospect of having to wait, will enter a guilty plea. Time and time again, Phil Vincent, a Perth lawyer who worked *pro bono* on a number of these cases in the 1990s, watched the same scene unfold in the courtroom. 'They'd file in, they would stand when they were told through an interpreter to stand, they would then have the charge read to them in the technical way that charges are always read, they would be asked whether they plead guilty or not guilty and usually to a man, they'd say "guilty".'[28]

Gani Pello pleaded guilty on his first arrest because he wanted to get home. 'We'd been thinking about our families. Who was going to buy food for them while we were in jail?' Yet when he was arrested a second time two years later, convinced of his innocence, he was adamant that he would never plead guilty. When it came time to leave Willie Creek for his day in court, the Fisheries officer who came to collect him told Gani he had to find and pay for a lawyer himself. 'How could I find a lawyer myself? How could I afford to pay a lawyer? I was a foreigner there. I didn't even have one rupiah in my hand.'[29] So he pleaded guilty, and went to prison for the next eighteen months. 'The only reason,' Gani believes, 'was I didn't have a lawyer to help me.'

In Darwin, the Northern Territory Legal Aid Office still has lawyers representing the Indonesian fishermen, but in Broome, in 1989, the West Australian Legal Aid Commission announced an end to the provision of legal assistance to Indonesian fishermen (although legal aid was still provided in some cases until 1996). Lack of funding was cited as the reason. There is no obligation for legal aid bodies to represent non-citizens in Australian courts.

The upshot of all this is that Indonesian fishermen who have no understanding of our legal system, combined with a general mistrust of the legal process, a tendency to plead guilty to get matters over with, and a future in jail, are unrepresented in West Australian courts. 'It is difficult to see how these defendants would be able to have a fair trial, as is a right before our courts.'[30]

It was this scenario that compelled Phil Vincent to work *pro bono* for the fishermen over a ten-year period from the late 1980s. It seemed to him a clear travesty of due process was occurring. But in the end, he stopped representing them. 'The system seemed to be in a sense so bad that almost by participating in the system you [were] condoning it and giving it a veneer of justice.'

Likewise Ted Wilkinson, a Broome Legal Aid lawyer for many years, believes that although lack of resources was the official reason that representation for the fishermen dried up, he couldn't see the point in propping up what was clearly a farcical situation. 'They do not speak English, have only their word against sophisticated Navy radar equipment, do not understand our system of law, and are destitute. It is, plainly speaking, a joke,' he concluded of Indonesian fishing trials. His presence in the courtroom, in his final opinion, only served to 'give a false impression of a fair trial'.[31]

Together with a *de facto* jail sentence, there is the added burden of the loss of their boats, and many fishermen have argued that this is by far the greater loss. Doused in petrol and set alight, boat-burnings are the most dramatic and brutal expression of the exercise of Australia's northern maritime sovereignty. In Darwin, they were until recently a public spectacle, and onlookers have been known to drape themselves in and wave Australian flags enthusiastically as the *perahu* explode in flames. At Willie Creek, it is a much more private affair. The fishermen are often made to douse and set fire to their own boats. They watch the flames with a mixture of despair and disbelief. The grief, especially among those who own their own boats, is palpable.

The destruction of one *perahu* impacts heavily not only on the fishermen but on the whole community. Given that most small *perahu* have seven to nine crew on board with families to support, its loss seriously jeopardises the livelihood of at least 30 to 40 people. Boat-burning is the Australian government's biggest weapon in the fight to deter Indonesian fishermen. 'I think this is [sic] the only real way we can deter them is to continually confiscate and burn their boats, so they lose all their boats and *all* their fishing equipment,' one West Australian Fisheries officer asserted in a radio interview in 1995.[32]

This is quite incredible, and an 'outright contradiction', in the words of Professor James Fox, an eastern Indonesia specialist. At a time when the Australian government is eager to be seen to be offering overseas aid to assist development of eastern Indonesia, it is also busily destroying the livelihood of some of its poorest inhabitants. Videotapes taken of boat-burnings in Darwin have even been sent back to Indonesia as a warning. Apart from the fact that the fishermen for whom the tapes are intended rarely, if ever, have access to video recorders, it is unlikely that such public exhibitions of boat-burnings would be interpreted as anything other than a hostile gesture.[33]

Forfeiture of boat, catch and equipment is now automatic upon apprehension. In the past, it was essentially a discretionary matter for the judge or magistrate, once a guilty charge had been proven. The new legislation, introduced in 1999, does provide for the owner of the boat to make a written claim within 30 days to the Fisheries Department. This then allows him to initiate proceedings against the Commonwealth within two months to recover his possessions. Indonesian fishermen are extremely unlikely to have the resources to initiate proceedings again the Commonwealth. In Darwin, some boat owners in Indonesia have been more active in taking this option, if the crew are first offenders and likely to get off with a good behaviour bond. Naturally, there needs to be a crew to sail the boat home. But in all other cases, forfeiture almost always occurs whether the fishermen are found guilty or not. This is fundamentally contrary to one of the basic principles of our legal system — the presumption of innocence.

A Broome Fisheries officer explained the rationale behind the recent legislative amendments. Firstly, sending a boat home was pointless, because 'it'd be back again in few more weeks, after it gets back to Indonesia'.[34] Secondly, the boats are considered unseaworthy by Australian standards and could be a quarantine risk, so they can't be sold on the local market. Another reason for forfeiture is to indirectly punish the boat owners who are, in his opinion, the real exploiters of the fishermen. However, even he conceded that this approach didn't seem to be working the way it was envisaged. It's amazing, he said, 'because we've actually asked them and said, of all the boats that we've seized over the last fifteen, twenty years from Pepela, has that reduced the number of boats in the area, and it hasn't . . . we're not really having a dent . . . on the vessel population at all'.

In fact, in the poorest communities like Pepela where fishermen do not usually own their own boats, forfeiture of the vessels is having the opposite of the intended effect on boat owners, who are profiting, not suffering from it. Fishermen operate as a collective. Every time boats and equipment are confiscated, the fishermen have to repay the owner for the loss. Anecdotal evidence collected from the fishermen and boat owners in Pepela put the value of a *perahu* at about 25 million rupiah. Sadli's debts are now in the vicinity of

3 million rupiah. He believes that for each arrest it takes three years of successful fishing to repay each debt. 'Even when I die,' Sadli told me, 'I will still have my debts.'

The destruction of a *perahu* is not only a huge economic loss, it is a spiritual one as well. 'A person can do wrong but their boat can't!' a Pepelan elder, Haji Hasan, remarked. To a fisherman, destruction of their boat is akin to a type of murder: 'When a *perahu* is apprehended and burnt until destroyed the builder experiences the feeling that the *perahu* is dead.'[35]

For the incarcerated fisherman, the heaviest burden is not knowing how their families will survive while they are away in prison. Johni said that although they were given enough food in jail, all they thought about was their families back home. 'I didn't know how they were . . . I felt like I wanted to die. I felt powerless. I thought I was going crazy.'

Pahang, a fisherman from the island of Mola, was distraught during his stay in Broome Prison. 'I just went to sea to get just enough money to buy food for these people,' he said, referring to his mother, three sisters and four nephews. 'That's why I feel like I am going mad because they put me in jail and I don't know what's going to happen [to them].' News Pahang received from another fisherman who joined him later in jail that his younger sister had just died increased his distress. 'I just want to die. Thinking of these people I left behind and one of them already dead. And if I die, who else is going to look after these people?'[36] Tragically Pahang died three months later, just after his release. I do not know the cause of his death.

The periods Indonesian fishermen are spending in prison are increasing, sometimes up to two or more years for repeat

offences. It is the women and children that do the time the
hardest. They often have no idea what has happened to their
sons, husbands or fathers when they don't come home at the
usual time. For all they know, their menfolk might have died
at sea. It isn't until word finally comes via another fisherman
returning home after completing his own jail term or, if a
fisherman is literate, by letter, that they learn of an arrest.
Meanwhile, they are left destitute. Agung was jailed for sixteen
months, and without him, his family was reduced to scaveng-
ing to survive. His grandmother walked 16 kilometres a day to
beg for rice. There are many stories such as these. These
women face impossible decisions. Many borrow more money
on top of the money originally borrowed by their menfolk
from the boat owner to support their families while they are
at sea. Debts quickly become astronomical and unmanageable.

Others find other husbands. Affliana, the young wife of
Matteos Tungga who was jailed for twenty months, found it
impossible to support her two children. In the end she was
forced to send them away to Matteos' parents on another
island. 'My husband gave me some money when he left, but
he borrowed that money. How could I pay it back? My child
was sick, I was sick too. I was going to send him a letter but
I didn't have enough money to buy the stamp.'[37] Affliana took
up with another man in the village. Johni's wife did too, and
he never saw her again. The last he heard of her and his small
child, they were living far away on another island. I visited
Matteos' parents in West Timor, and met Matteos and
Affliana's two young girls. 'They are like orphans,' Matteos'
father told me. 'Sometimes they sing a song asking for their
parents to come back.'[38]

Fathers return home to find they are strangers to their
children, or that they have missed their births altogether.
Peter Isak Husein told me his biggest regret about his time
spent in jail was missing the birth of his youngest daughter.

'She has suffered since she was born because at that time I wasn't with her. I was in jail, I couldn't feed her.' When Gani returned home, the three-month-old daughter he had left behind had turned two. 'She had grown so much,' he said. 'She could talk. She could say mum and dad. But she didn't know her father. I don't know how I can make her get used to me. We have just met again, so she is still quite scared of me.' Worse, children die, either from hunger-related or preventable diseases. Both Ted Wilkinson and Jill Elliott were privy to situations where fishermen received news that family members had died. 'The amount of children that were dying was incredible', Elliott said. 'I mean we've got to take some responsibility for that.'

Frank Harkin, superintendent of Broome Prison for over ten years and with over 30 years' experience in the West Australian correctional services, witnessed the gradual whittling way of Indonesian inmates' rights in relation to prison gratuities. In the beginning, in the late 1980s and early 1990s, he had paid the fishermen in accordance with what every other prisoner was paid in line with the work they were doing. But against his wishes, he was eventually ordered by his superiors to pay them only at the lowest rate of prison pay, regardless of the work they were doing. 'At the time I argued against it because it meant that for the first time, to my knowledge, a group of prisoners were being treated differently by legislation.'[39] He wasn't sure what it was meant to achieve. 'I suspect it was purely punitive and didn't have any rationale in the sense of a justice system.'

Despite this, the idea that Indonesian fishermen deliberately get arrested to get rich in Australian jails has provided fertile ground for politicians and journalists wishing to make political mileage out of their presence on the Australian border and in Australian jails. From the late 1980s through to the late 1990s, cartoons in the pages of the *West Australian* depicted the fishermen deliberately getting arrested: 'Three more years on prison pay and I'll be able to afford my own boat', one caption read, alongside an ugly caricature of a grinning, bag-laden Indonesian.[40] Another showed Australian officials greeting an Indonesian fishing boat with the words, 'Shall we carry your bags sir?' A sign at the top of the cartoon read: 'Your car and jet await you.'[41]

It's a common theme, and not just in the cartoons. Demonising the Indonesian fishermen was also something the West Australian Labor MP, Senator Jim McKiernan, practised in the pages of his local newspaper. In a letter headed 'Standing Up for the Australian Taxpayer', he asked, rhetorically:

> Do Indonesian fishers and people smugglers return time after time again to Australia even after being convicted and given prison sentences? Are they paid while in prison? Do they purchase consumer goods with the monies earned in prison and bring these goods back to Indonesia with them when they are deported at the end of their sentence?[42]

The answer to the last question, at least, is no. Indonesian fishermen are not allowed to keep any of the money they earn in prison, nor to return home with goods they might have bought with prison wages earned during their sentence. Gani, jailed for eighteen months, received many letters from his young wife asking for help: 'Every time she sent me a letter she said she needed some money. There was nothing I could send her . . . when I returned home, I was grateful that my family was still alive.' Johni earned $13 a week for work in prison, and couldn't use any of it to help his family. Yet these men have proven an easy target for accusations of opportunism, fueled by their popular image as heinous criminals, given their alien origins and their inability to defend themselves. Trespasser, pariah, plunderer — there could hardly be any labels more damning in the contemporary Australian vocabulary than these.

Agung spent sixteen months making bricks and working in the kitchen in an Australian jail. He remembers what happened when it came time to go home to Indonesia:

> Immigration picked us up and said that they had to seize our stuff. They were afraid if we brought home some stuff from Australia we would sell it in Indonesia and use the money to buy a boat to return to Australia. I told them that we couldn't possibly buy a boat by selling this stuff. They said we were lying . . . we were afraid of them so we didn't do anything.

Nevertheless, one typically misleading and ludicrous television news item showed a stack of televisions and stereo systems at the airport, accompanying a story about the repatriation of Indonesian fishermen at the end of their prison term.

Philip Ruddock explained the rationale behind the confiscation of money or goods in response to a query made by the fishermen via the Human Rights and Equal Opportunity Commission in May 1998:

> The costs of your removal are your responsibility and you remain liable for the repayment of this debt along with any costs while in immigration detention. If you are unwilling or unable to pay any of these costs, officers of the Department are empowered to seize any of your cash or property to be used as payment towards your debt.[43]

Upon release, the fishermen are flown straight to Denpasar airport. They are given, on paper at least, $40 each, although many I spoke to said they only received $20, to return home. The distance from Bali to Rote, and to other islands in Sulawesi from which most of the fishermen originate, is over 1000 kilometres. To Pepela, it is a three to four day journey, and at least two ferry rides, via Kupang. The money barely covers the cost of one ferry ride. The ferry from Bali departs infrequently, and often the fishermen have to sleep on the streets in Bali for anything up to two weeks. To them, Bali is a foreign country. The language, religion, local government and culture differ markedly from their own. Every fisherman who has experienced it mentions the landing in Bali as a particularly harsh aspect of their sentence. Agung said that the group he was with didn't know whether they needed letters of permission to travel from Denpasar, where to sleep or how to get help.

There have been reports of some fishermen never making it home. Gani slept on the streets in Bali for five days before he could get a ferry to Kupang. Sadli was forced to beg for food. Others approach the welfare office in Denpasar to try to get some assistance, but these resources are already stretched for local residents so they rarely have much luck. For the Australian officers who escort them, on the other hand, the trip is a good chance to get some duty-free shopping done in Bali. 'I don't mind taking them because I get to buy the missus some duty free, and get my own in too. I just drop them off, shop and get on a plane home,' one officer quipped at Broome airport.[44]

Sadli said he looked around when they got off the plane, but strangely, 'the Australian officer who escorted us didn't hand us to the Indonesian immigration or the local government, he just disappeared'. Within the space of an hour, Sadli was approached by some men who 'offered us a lot of money if we could escort some people from the Middle East to Australia'. Sadli resisted the offer, although there are no doubt others who, faced with the debt-ridden future of their return, have proven more susceptible. Like Hanafi Laduma:

> We are poor fishermen . . . Since way before, our parents were fishermen so we too became fishermen. Over the last year we haven't been able to make ends meet in our households . . . we have been forced, out of necessity, to take people to Ashmore Reef. With the little bit of money that this brought we forgot about the prospect of jail in Australia because it was a matter of survival.[45]

Hanafi is from Pepela, but he wrote this from his prison cell in Western Australia. Taking people to Ashmore Reef is only the latest chapter in the history of the Rotenese relationship to the place they once called their 'garden in the sea'. For the Indonesian fishermen, Ashmore Reef has long been a worksite, a shelter, a place to teach their young, a burial ground, a precious watering hole in the middle of the ocean. Australia's Ashmore Reef is a troubled border outpost, the last gate in its fortifications against intrusion. The Ashmore Reef story is the wider Australian story of possession and the Rotenese story of loss.

STONE FENCES AND
SAD STORIES

Ashmore Reef

ASHMORE REEF IS made up of three small sand islands, each harbouring a few sandbanks and lagoons, and surrounded by a fringing reef. It is approximately 190 nautical miles from the Australian mainland and about 78 nautical miles from Rote. From the air it is quite beautiful. Incredible turquoise waters sketch the contours of the islands, framed by the darker blue of the open sea. The sandy surface is scattered with native grasses and low-lying bushes. Among environmentalists the reef is famous for harbouring the largest variety of sea snakes in the world and as a staging post for huge numbers of migratory birds. The islands are also a feeding and breeding ground for turtles, and a critical habitat for dugong.

Ashmore Reef got its name from Captain Samuel Ashmore, who sighted the reef in 1811. A year earlier he had sighted and named Hibernia Reef after his ship the *Hibernia*. Other reefs and islands in the Timor Sea also bear the names of minor figures and their ships in nineteenth-century European navigation. Cartier Island, 25 nautical miles to the southeast of Ashmore Reef, was named by Captain Nash who sighted it from the *Cartier* in 1800. Scott Reef was named by the British Captain Heywood on a surveying expedition of northwest Australia in 1801, and Browse Island was named in 1838 by Captain Browse, who stumbled upon the island on a journey between Rote and the Kimberley coastline. In 1842 Seringapatam Reef was named after a sighting by the crew of the *Seringapatam*.

Dutch colonial reports from Indonesia detail evidence of early Indonesian fishing voyages to the reef, possibly as early as 1700, as well as its use as a staging post on the way to the coastline of northern Australia. Matthew Flinders first heard of the existence of Ashmore Reef after his contact with the Malay fleets along the north coast of Australia at the turn of the nineteenth century. Making inquiries during his sojourn in Kupang (Dutch Timor), he heard how the 'natives of Macassar had long been accustomed to fish for trepang among the islands in the vicinity of Java, and upon a dry shoal to the south of Rotte'. They had found the reef by accident, having been swept there by the northwest monsoon.[1]

His information accords with the Rotenese story of discovery. 'It was in fact people from Rote who discovered Pulau Pasir about 300 years ago,' Sadli began. Both his grandfathers, ninth-generation Rotenese fishermen, had told him the story of discovery of the place they called *Pulau Pasir*, Sand Island, or *Nusa Solokaek* in the local Rotenese language. Rotenese traders returning from a trip to Kupang to barter sugar got caught in a storm. It was the month of February, and the winds were too powerful to resist. They drifted for six days and six nights, 'until one morning they saw lots of birds from Pulau Pasir, lots and lots of birds, which made them think these birds must have a home'. They followed them, and soon the surface of the water glowed a bright green. They had stumbled upon an island. 'But they were surprised. Why was there an island here made of sand without any mountains?'

The sailors called the first island they came to from the west Pulau Satu, or First Island, the second Pulau Dua, or Second Island and the last, Pulau Tiga, Third Island. They discovered, after digging for water on all three islands, that the water on the middle island was the least salty and the most drinkable. From that time onwards, Ashmore Reef became a popular watering hole for trepangers on their way to the northwest coast of Australia or for those scouring the seabeds closer to home. They planted coconuts on Pulau Dua and Pulau Tiga to signal where drinkable water could be found. There are still two or three coconut palms standing on Pulau Dua near the well.

They waited day after day for a wind to set sail. Finally, they decided to try for home. Ahmad Hadem, Sadli's maternal grandfather, took the helm and steered the boat towards a constellation of three stars. The next mornings, the birds were again in front of them. They realised that in order to get home, they had to sail with these three stars at their back. Stars move quickly. One person had to watch the stars all night to make sure they were always behind the boat. A month had passed by the time the fishermen arrived back in Rote. To prove the existence of the island in the middle of the open sea, the sailors had brought back with them birds' eggs they had collected.[2]

Another Rotenese story of discovery tells how four elders, or lords as they are known in Rotenese lore, built a large *perahu* and set out in search of new knowledge. Their destination was Batavia, the home of the Dutch East India

Company, whose colonial presence in Indonesia was known in Rote but their origins were a mystery. They intended to head north, but a wind swept them south, all the way to Ashmore Reef. One of the lords, Foe Mpura, took a stick, carved his name in it and stuck it in the sand.[3]

—

It was well over a century after Indonesian seafarers started going there that Ashmore Reef first came to European notice. The discovery of guano (bird droppings), in the 1870s attracted first the Americans, then the British. There was considerable friction between the two camps over the guano deposits, at the time favoured for its amazing fertilising properties, but it was Britain who eventually annexed the reef in 1878. This was formalised in 1906. In spite of Foe Mpura's stick in the sand, the 206 crew members of the British ship *Cambrian* hoisted the Union Jack, fired a 21-gun salute and sang a rousing rendition of the national anthem.[4] Guano mining ended in 1904, but not before extensive environmental damage had been inflicted on the reef.

Motivated by a desire to attach its isolated and far-flung possessions around the world to more substantial parts of the Crown colonies, Britain handed sovereignty of Ashmore Reef over to the Commonwealth of Australia in 1931.[5] The transfer to Western Australia was formalised in 1934. For the next 50-odd years, the reef remained largely a piece of paper shuffled between state and federal government departments. From the West Australians the reef was passed on to the Common-wealth, and in 1938 was handed over to the Northern Ter-ritory, where it remained until 1978 when the Northern Territory gained self-government. After this, Ashmore Reef and its neighbouring island, Cartier, were returned to the Commonwealth. In 1983 the Australian government declared

Ashmore Reef a national nature reserve. Cartier Island was declared a national marine reserve on 21 June 2000 and closed to Indonesian fishermen.

Despite the fact that Ashmore Reef was included in the original MOU Box, its special designation as a nature reserve has meant that the usual rules of access for traditional Indonesian fishermen no longer apply. They are prohibited from entering the reef except to seek emergency shelter from storms and are allowed to collect drinking water only at one lagoon on West Island. They are otherwise barred altogether. This has caused considerable upset because, as Sadli explains in his story of discovery, 'years passed and generations passed and the [Rotenese fishermen] regarded Pulau Pasir as part of their own land'.[6] Haji Hasan, a respected elder in Pepela, was more forceful. 'We've been earning our living there all this time. Even though Australia forbids us to go there, we'll still go because we can't not go there. We must go.'[7]

Australian environmentalists and government officials defend the expulsion, in the main, by arguing that Indonesian fishermen wreak substantial environmental damage. The scientific concerns associated with fishing at the reef are based on fears that regular over-exploitation of clams, various molluscs and holothurians damages the continued biological diversity and life of the reef. Trochus and trepang are said to be heavily depleted on most reefs in the MOU Box area. Moreover, many of the species Indonesian fishermen are accused of targeting are protected under the *Environmental Protection and Biodiversity Conservation Act (1999)*. There are over 40 species of sea and migratory birds listed as being protected at Ashmore, as well as sea snakes, turtles, dugong and all cetaceans.[8] Reports of bird slaughter have been widespread, and the killing of dugong and turtles for food. A senior Fisheries officer remembered the days before the reef was a nature reserve. 'There were so many of the birds flying in the air and they were within a few foot of your head, and [the Indonesian fishermen] they'd have a . . . stick, and they'd just whack the birds and they'd bring them down . . . and that was to get red meat I suppose.'[9] Fishermen also took eggs.

Sadli vehemently disputes the charge of environmental vandalism. For Australians to say 'that the Rote people are always killing birds, that's simply not true'. The birds of Pulau Pasir are both the saviours and the guides of Rotenese fishermen. When the original Rotenese crew who discovered the island came home with birds' eggs, they told the people that in the future, when fishing at Pulau Pasir, 'if they want to eat they must only take a little and must not destroy the mother birds, because then they would not be able to help them again'. The Rotenese insist that if too many birds were killed, 'it wasn't Rote people who killed them'. Given that the Rotenese have been visitors to the island for well over two centuries at least, this makes sense.

But Rotenese fishermen are not the only ones now fishing in the region, and the increase in numbers has undoubtedly put greater pressures on the island. There are conflicting reports about whether birds on Ashmore are under threat. But the outline of the dispute between the Rotenese fishermen and Australian environmentalists is a familiar one in many parts of the world. The encounters between traditional societies and nation states have forced a breakdown in the old, customary rules that once governed tenures of land and sea. From the Rotenese perspective, the misguided and ill-worded Australian legislation determining access doesn't distinguish between those who would once have been the custodians of the reefs and waters, and newcomers without the same sort of ecological knowledge or care.

The 'tragedy of the commons' theory is widely believed in the West to have universal validity. This theory, first developed by the biologist Garrett Hardin, assumes that people will always put individual gain ahead of long-term sustainability. Where there is open access to resources, Hardin argued, human nature will always dictate unlimited exploitation to the point of destruction.[10] Because humans left to their own devices couldn't be trusted, the only solution was increased bureaucratic regulation of individual behaviour.

What Hardin's approach ignored, however, was the existence of other patterns of regulation and rules of behaviour operating outside the capitalist work ethic. Traditional methods of ecological preservation have operated in fishing communities for centuries. Since the 1970s, the existence of dynamic community-based systems of marine tenure that practise ecological preservation by regulating access to fishing grounds has been documented around the world, including eastern Indonesia. 'Our ancestors always told us not to take more fish than we needed so there would always be plenty for future generations,' the Rotenese fishermen say.[11] Indiscriminate methods of fishing are not in their interests, nor their custom. 'How would damaging the reef benefit us?'[12]

Conservationists accuse the fishermen of a 'slash and burn' approach, of plundering, not protecting, finite resources. They equate the fishermen's activities with vandalism, excess and cruelty. It's a perception of indigenous activity repeated in many colonial settler societies. In her examination of European wildlife conservation in Africa, for example, Jane Carruthers found that from the outset whites saw African hunting traditions as barbaric and ruthless, and blamed Africans for the extermination of wildlife. The creation of the national parks and game reserves facilitated the expulsion of the African hunters from their customary hunting grounds.[13]

James Fox notes that it 'is only when these systems collide with national and international legal structures that the traditions regulating access are overwhelmed'.[14] In recent years the fact that these methods have become disrupted in the traditional fisheries of the Timor Sea is not in dispute, but it is uncertain to what extent Australia's policies in the region have contributed to the problem. For example, the restriction of Indonesian fishermen to a reduced area, and the increase in fishermen claiming to be 'traditional' by simple virtue of boats without motors, are both problems stemming from Australian legislation. What is certain, however, is that the fishermen of Rote face exactly the same issue of resource degradation by outsiders, whether it be other impoverished neighbours encroaching on their traditional waters, or commercial interests. Their dependence on the sustainability of a particular resource is driven by real-life questions of survival. Their loss is more immediate, less altruistic, an altogether different loss to that of the Western conservationist.

The movement to protect parts of the world, to fence them off from the corrupting influence of human endeavour, has been largely motivated by a desire for wilderness. Wilderness is imagined as existing in some pure, idyllic state, unadulterated by a human presence. It is, ultimately, a myth, 'an invention of civilised man'.[15] There is no such thing as non-human landscapes. But in the pursuit of this green aesthetic, this desire to protect nature by restoring it to its original, pure state, assiduous attempts have been made to remove anything that might detract from or corrupt the wilderness ideal. The eradication of culture in the rescue and rebirth of wilderness is a complicated procedure. David Lowenthal has written about how all traces of seventeenth- and eighteenth-century cultivation were removed in the creation of a new national park in the Virgin Islands 'so as to restore a "wilderness" landscape'.[16]

In the Australian case of the Langwarrin military reserve in Victoria, its transformation into the Langwarrin Flora and

Fauna Reserve in 1985 involved removing any signs of its early military history because they contradicted the aim of a flora and fauna reserve.[17] But at Ashmore Reef the signs of previous visitation by Indonesian fishermen have been retained for their archaeological value. Graves, earthenware pottery and stoneware, wells, coconut palms and cooking sites are all now listed in the Environment Australia (previously Australian National Parks and Wildlife Service) management plan for the reef as adding to its heritage status. Here, culture is preserved as testimony to a primitive past, rather than an active present. The fishermen are denied access, even as their traces are turned into historical relics. Their contemporary killing-off is also part of the rebirthing process.

But the fishermen of Rote believe they have inalienable rights to the islands, and still refer to Ashmore Reef as their 'garden' or 'field'. 'Besides feeling angry, we also feel that this is unfair,' said Haji Hasan. 'Fishermen from Rote think that the island belongs to Indonesia because it is so close to Rote Island. Pulau Pasir is our backyard. That is why we go there all the time.'[18] When I asked Sadli why Pulau Pasir was so significant, he told me the story of the stone fences. 'When I was a kid, I used to ask my grandfather many questions, such as how did he get to Pulau Pasir, who took him there, what did he use to catch fish?' His grandfather told him they made stone fences, arranging the stones to make a fish trap, shaking palm leaves at the open end of the trap to stop the fish escaping. They then threw grated coconut into the water. This made the water very oily and very clear. 'They could even see the fish that were hiding under the rocks in the water [to spear them]. Those stone fences still remain . . . we Rote people call them *lutu*.' They are a piece of Rotenese history, he told me, not Australian.

There are also Indonesian graves on Ashmore Reef. There are at least six, clearly marked, on West Island, grouped together under a coconut palm. They are carefully laid out, two of the graves marked with a coral perimeter and painted wooden posts with names and dates. Another grave has a flat rounded piece of coral rock as a headstone. One grave on Middle Island is even more elaborate, its base constructed of small coral rocks, smoothed by a whitewash coating of lime paste. It has two wooden markers at each end. Despite the restrictions on access, this grave appears to be tended on a regular basis, every two or three years. Recently, a number of much older, unmarked graves were exposed by the weather, the skeletal remains eventually washed out to sea.[19]

Visiting the graves on Ashmore Reef was once an integral part of every fishing expedition. In theory, fishermen are still allowed to visit the graves — but only if accompanied by an Australian official. In practice, it is unlikely that many are aware of this exception to the rule, and fishermen continue to visit the graves to pay respect to their dead. 'We don't go to Pulau Pasir only to fish,' Agung explained. 'Some of our sad stories are kept there.' Fishermen bring flowers and pray at the graves before starting work. Gani witnessed on many occasions families going on special trips together to visit the graves. 'I myself saw some graves of people from Sulawesi. Their families went to the graves to pray for them. They poured some perfume and left some cigarettes and other things.'

Australian officers discovered the existence of a fresh grave on Cartier Island in 2000. A rusted metal pole together with sand, rock and a wooden plank marked the site. Three days after the discovery, a special team flew to the island, dug up the grave and transported the remains to Darwin. The body was autopsied, and aside from locating the age of the fisherman as somewhere between 25 and 35, no other identification was made. The body was re-buried in an unmarked grave in Darwin's Thorak Cemetery. It may be difficult at first to comprehend why Australia would engage in such an expensive exercise. But once we begin to examine the politics of conservation and the relationship between conservation and sovereignty, it begins to make more sense.

Under international law, sovereignty can only be maintained by effective occupation or proven and continuous administration of a territory. Thus, uninhabited islands present a problem; and uninhabited islands closer to Indonesia than Australia, and with significantly stronger links with 'foreigners' such as Indonesian fishermen, particularly so. In 1985, Henry Burmester, a specialist in maritime law at the Australian National University, noted that 'in recent years Australia has begun to pay more attention to its island territories . . . and has begun to recognise the considerable maritime rights that small islands can bring'. He explicitly outlined the problem in relation to the Ashmore and Cartier islands:

> Australian sovereignty could be increasingly questioned if Indonesian fishermen in large numbers were allowed regularly to occupy, build graves, and interfere with the island wildlife. [Unlike other island possessions] Ashmore and Cartier are located in an area where another country has a particular interest and concern. If Australia seriously wishes to retain this island territory considerable resources will have to be made available to enable a continual assertion and display of its sovereignty to be made.[20]

Seen in this light, the removal of the body from Cartier was a logical exercise in the 'assertion and display' of Australia's sovereignty. The fact that it was a recent grave might also explain why the body was chosen to be removed, as a strong message to the fishermen. Burmester reminded his readers of a statement by a Mr Hawker MP in 1938:

> It is our duty to see that Australian possession is
> effective, and not merely latent, lest it be later disputed
> by foreigners who might claim to have established some
> sort of rights to the island.[21]

The location of Ashmore and Cartier Reefs, recently renamed
Ashmore and Cartier Islands, right on the margin of Australia's
territorial limits, is undoubtedly significant in strategic terms.
Moreover, since the Timor Sea has become a zone for the
accumulation of capital, increased attention has focused on
ensuring the effective possession of its islands. Making these
islands nature reserves achieves this end. It has facilitated the
expulsion of the Indonesian fishermen. It has also created a
strong administrative presence — Environment Australia
personnel, Customs officers, scientists, archaeologists and the
like — all adding up to a constant watch. At the same time,
their new conservation status has reinvented these far-flung
reefs as sacred Australian places. It has morally anchored them
to the nation state, where previously they held only political
status as territorial acquisitions.

In fact, many of the islands dotting the entire cir-
cumference of the Australian maritime estate are protected
nature reserves. Some of these are also, paradoxically, sites of
substantial mining interests. Petroleum companies have been
investigating the commercial potential of Ashmore and
Cartier Islands for some time. Oil and gas exploration wells
have been drilled in the vicinity of the reserves, and there are
currently permits for further exploration issued to the east and
southeast of the islands. Cartier Reef and the surrounding
area, within a 10-kilometre radius, is also now a gazetted
Australian Defence Practice Area for military exercises, and
used as an air weapons range. The potential threats to the reef
environment associated with increased shipping, rig and
pipeline construction, possible oil spills, drilling or military

practice have not, to date, been investigated. In light of the concerns about the damaging impact of Indonesian fishermen, this seems rather odd.

———

Ashmore Reef catapulted into mainstream Australian consciousness in the late 1990s. It became famous not for its oil and gas, but for the people that started turning up on its sand banks. In 1995 two small wooden *perahu* turned up at Ashmore Reef, carrying a total of eleven passengers. On one boat there was a family of five Afghanis; on the other, six Kurds from Turkey, all of them exhausted by months of desperate hardship and uncertainty, their immense relief tinged with the barest puzzlement at reaching this barren sandbank on the other side of the world called Australia. The crews politely handed them over to the Customs vessel stationed at the reef, turned around and sailed home again. The travellers were eventually given refugee status. At the time their arrival caused barely a ripple in the nation's media. But these two boats were the harbingers of a different type of traffic on this old sea route. A new commodity was being traded in the Timor Sea.

From that moment onwards, wooden boats, many of them traditional *perahu*, all of them carrying scared and exhausted passengers, began to wash up on the reef with increasing regularity. In 1999, 47 vessels carrying a total of 1398 people used Ashmore Reef as a point of entry to Australia. Dramatic images of people stranded at the reef flashed regularly across TV screens as news bulletins trumpeted the sudden surge in refugees coming to Australia by boat. A new discovery for most Australians at the beginning of the 1990s, by decade's end Ashmore Reef was a household word.

For the asylum seekers, Ashmore Reef was the final staging post on the 'people smuggling' trade route to Australia and the first step inside the borders of the new country. But in 2001, the federal government responded to the arrivals by rewriting the reef's political status. Under the *Migration Amendment (Excision From Migration Zone) Act (2001)*, Ashmore and Cartier Islands were 'excised' from the Australian 'migration zone'. Christmas Island, Cocos (Keeling) Island and various offshore installations were also redefined as 'excised offshore places'. Until this time, there had been no separation of a 'migration zone' from Australia's sovereign borders. Boat people who landed at Ashmore could heave a sigh of relief that they had reached Australia, even though it was another 200 miles to the mainland.

The very term 'excision' was revealing. It evoked the idea of a surgical procedure, of cutting out irritating, cancerous sores from the healthy body of the nation. A year later, in December 2002, the Howard Government was still seeking to have 3000 more islands excised, a move that was blocked by the Senate. Jokes were made that Tasmania was next. The arbitrary use of new border protection powers was exposed on 18 December 2002 when ABC Radio National's *AM* news program revealed that over the weekend Immigration Minister Philip Ruddock had secretly ordered the excision of another four islands off the coast of Western Australia. 'It was an attempt to catch what was thought to be a boatload of asylum seekers, to stop them from claiming refugee status on Australian soil, but it turned out to be only a fishing boat,' the journalist said. 'Now Mr Ruddock is quickly moving to rescind the regulations excising the islands from Australia's migration zone but he says that he would do the same again.'[22]

This *ad hoc* approach demonstrates the fluidity of the Australian map. Excising Ashmore Reef added to the sense that out there, at sea, Australia's edges start to fray and unravel. It was also a potent metaphor for the way the asylum seekers who landed there were cast adrift by mainland Australia. Under the new border protection legislation, those who landed at Ashmore Reef became 'offshore entry persons', instead of the previous title of 'unauthorised arrivals'. What this meant in effect was that anyone who washed up on Ashmore Reef or any other excised place, even if found later to be a genuine refugee, was automatically denied the right to apply to stay, even temporarily. Like the reef itself, the people who arrived there became the nation's cast-offs.

Governed by a security agenda and an environmental agenda, with its joint status of protected nature reserve and excised territory, Ashmore Reef represents both the fragility and threat associated with Australia's borders. The discourses and practices of environmental protection and border pro-tection are very similar. Both describe danger and exclusivity. Both are designed to safeguard precious places from un-welcome peoples. Nor is the relationship between the two necessarily coincidental. In an interesting twist, the search for boat people in the Timor Sea was listed under 'environmental expenditure' in the 2002 federal budget. An article in the *Sydney Morning Herald* pointed out that this had included a $243 million item for maritime policing of illegal fishermen and asylum seekers.[23]

Andrew Stafford is a birdwatcher who made a rare visit to Ashmore Reef in late October 2001. There were seven other equally ardent birdlovers along for the eight-day chartered cruise. They were startled out of their avian reveries when they passed within 100 metres of a refugee boat near the reef. From the deck of their luxury boat, they watched as the vessel listed so far to port, it seemed about to collapse. Barely 17 metres long, it was 'heaving under a weight of piled-up humanity, possessions and unnameable detritus'. The birdwatchers were told by the Customs and naval officers guarding the boat that the asylum seekers were being encouraged to return to international waters. 'Encouraged,' Stafford remarked, 'seemed a generous euphemism.'[24] The boat was eventually sent back out to sea. What struck Stafford was that for most Australians, Ashmore Reef was so far away that it barely seemed part of home. 'The desperation and degradation endured by those who seek shelter in its waters remain equally remote from Australian psyches.'

When Gani made his discovery of the reef as a young boy, it signified a moment of great importance. 'I wanted to know how life was as a fisherman in the ocean. I told my father that I wanted to join him fishing, no matter how hard it would be.' He was thirteen when his father finally agreed to take him, and they sailed directly to Pulau Pasir. Gani was astonished by what he saw. 'I didn't understand how this island could be situated in the middle of this beautiful ocean.' His father took him to other islands, but nothing could eclipse the unique beauty of Pasir. The journey marked a turning point. A year later, he became a fisherman in his own right.

It's a sad irony that the vast majority of its Australian owners have never visited Ashmore Reef and never will, and have little idea of where it really is. What most do know, however, is that it is Australia's test site of its sovereignty, the gatepost hung with the 'do not enter' sign.

An aerial photograph shows a number of people marooned on a thin strip of sand in the middle of the ocean, waving frantically up at the camera, a rough construction of blue plastic tarpaulins on the beach behind them. In the foreground a dilapidated wooden boat lies bleaching under the harsh sun.[25] It's a desperate scene. This is the Ashmore

Reef that most Australians are familiar with — a miserable, godforsaken no man's land, a place of remoteness and pathos. It shares nothing with the Rotonese Pulau Pasir. They couldn't be further apart.

FORTRESS AUSTRALIA

Border protection in the
Timor Sea

FROM 1995, ASYLUM SEEKERS, the vast majority of them from the Middle East, began boarding *perahu* in eastern Indonesia to make the last leg of their journey to Australia. For the Indonesian crews it was easy money — a quick trip to Ashmore Reef, a day from Rote, two from Kupang if the conditions were right. Payment was promised on return, as much as could be made in a month or more of fishing. At first, operations were small, the boats carrying anywhere between four and sixteen people. In four years, 118 asylum seekers arrived at the reef this way. But in 1999 these numbers escalated sharply. New organisers took over the operations, replacing small *perahu* with large wooden ferries, many of them rotting with disuse and ill-repair. Inexperienced crews made up of farmers or itinerant labourers began to take the place of skilled Indonesian sailors. Hundreds of people were crammed onto open decks and into suffocating holds without air, light or water, where they were choked by diesel fumes, and tossed about violently by storms.

During the next two years, thousands of asylum seekers turned up in the Timor Sea, earning these waters a front-row place in Australia's newly designated 'arc of instability'.[1] By the turn of the twenty-first century, invasion anxiety had reached fever pitch, fuelled by the crude rhetoric of politicians who claimed, among other things, that these numbers — actually tiny in comparison with most of the rest of the world — constituted a national emergency. Six years after the first group of refugees was delivered to Australian authorities at Ashmore Reef, the population awoke to the by-now familiar news that they were being swamped and the borders were at breaking point under the strain. 'Our open-door borders: How guns, drugs and people are swamping the nation's barely protected coastline' ran the front-page headline of *The Australian*.[2] Underneath, another heading read 'FORTRESS AUSTRALIA UNDER ATTACK'. The news team was there, in the air above Ashmore Reef, to spot the eighteenth boat to arrive at the 'taxi rank' that year. The next morning, the MV *Tampa* sailed into the maelstrom.

⟶

The *Tampa* was a Norwegian container ship, one of the biggest roll-on, roll-off vessels in the world. It departed Fremantle bound for Singapore on 23 August 2001. It was still in the Indian Ocean three days later when an emergency distress call went out to ships in the vicinity of a sinking wooden boat. The *Palapa* was carrying 433 asylum seekers, the majority of them from Afghanistan. It was 20 metres long and in bad shape. Holes in the hull were being stuffed up with plastic bags. The passengers had just spent a terrible night weathering a violent storm. The fact that they were still afloat the next day was little short of a miracle. The deck was awash with blood, vomit and urine. The wheelhouse was breaking apart. That morning the *Palapa* was spotted dead in the water by Australian Coastwatch on a routine surveillance flight, but it took another eighteen hours before Australian Search and Rescue (AusSAR) put out the emergency call. The *Tampa*, under the captaincy of Arne Rinnan, responded, transferring the distressed passengers aboard.[3]

Sadly for the passengers of the *Palapa*, their timing could hardly have been worse. Fear and insecurity dominated the politics of an election campaign in full swing. The *Tampa* lobbed straight into the path of a government in need of nothing short of a miracle to prove to a sceptical public that it was in control. The media was saturated with talk of a major refugee crisis. The revival of dormant invasion anxieties had renewed old fears of an 'unguarded coastline' and the 'empty north'. The Howard Government swung into action. The *Tampa* inched its laborious, ungainly way across the television screens of millions of people around the globe to the brittle war tune of a government in full military regalia.

The American television network CNN compared the *Tampa* with the 'voyage of the damned', the tragic journey of the Jewish refugees in search of a safe country in which to escape Hitler's tyranny. Australians might have recalled the *Afghan*. In 1888, this ship and three others were also refused permission to land. Nearly 600 Chinese passengers waited on board in Sydney Harbour for weeks, vainly hoping to be granted permission to come ashore. People lined the wharf to fling abuse at the 'yellow skinned' impostors, while inside the hallowed halls of the New South Wales parliament, politicians hotly debated the introduction of a *Chinese Restriction Bill*. The Chinese watched the crowd from their ship in the harbour, their hopes of safe passage evaporating as the weeks passed grimly by.[4]

The decision not to allow the Chinese immigrants to land was clearly illegal given the absence of any restrictive immigration legislation. 'I cast to the winds your permits of exemption,' a defiant premier announced to the House. 'I care nothing about your cobwebs of technical law; I am obeying a law far superior to the law which issued these [entry] permits; namely, the law of the preservation of society in New South Wales.'[5] For Henry Parkes, the fight to protect Australia against Asian intruders was paramount. The *Chinese Restriction and Regulation Act 1888 (NSW)* was quickly passed to apply retrospectively to defend the government's actions. Finally, defeated, the ship returned to Hong Kong. In the words of George Dibb, the whole affair resembled 'a sudden spasm of fear and panic'.[6]

Over a 110 years later, the *Tampa* became John Howard's *Afghan*. 'These people will never set foot on Australian soil . . . never,' the prime minister declared, on the day that the *Tampa* began to make its way towards Christmas Island in Australian territorial waters. The *Tampa* had originally made for the nearest Indonesian port of call, Merak, but at the forceful request of a number of the passengers who threatened to begin throwing themselves overboard if they were taken back to Indonesia, had turned around. The *Tampa*'s imminent approach into Australian waters was conveyed to Canberra, where the matter was immediately taken out of the hands of the Department of Immigration and Multicultural and Indigenous Affairs (DIMIA), and into those of the prime minister and his advisors. The *Tampa* was refused permission to enter Australian waters.

Licensed to carry 50 people, and now holding 500, many of them ill, the *Tampa* was no longer legally seaworthy. Christmas Island was the closest port. In these circumstances, Captain Arne Rinnan refused to comply with Canberra's request to leave Australian waters. While the situation on board his ship deteriorated by the hour, the *Tampa* remained marooned outside the 12 nautical mile limit. The Royal Flying Doctor Service, who had spoken with the captain and first officer of the *Tampa*, informed AusSAR's Rescue Coordination that of the 438 people on board, fifteen were unconscious. There was a sick child, one person with a broken leg, and a large number of people with open sores and skin infections. There were a number of pregnant women on board. The adults had begun a hunger strike. Many were suffering abdominal pains, diarrhoea and dehydration. The temperature on board was sweltering. The only toilet facilities were buckets separated by wooden partitions in an empty shipping container. At this point, the Royal Flying Doctor Service assessed that there was a 'mass situation medical crisis and that medical attention was urgently required'.[7]

At first the Howard Government largely ignored, or at least downplayed, the emergency calls for assistance, instead accusing the captain of lying about the medical situation on board.[8] In the end, Australia sent its own military doctor to the ship with a team of Special Air Service (SAS) troops. He examined all 438 people on board within one hour (43 minutes to be exact) and apparently concluded that no one was in a serious condition. 'He must be a superman. We don't have any kind of that doctor in Norway,' a spokesman for the Norwegian foreign minister commented dryly.[9]

Eventually, after four days, the *Tampa* pushed into Australian territorial waters, making its third mayday signal of distress. A few hours later, 45 SAS troops boarded the *Tampa* and took control of the ship. International condemnation was swift and harsh. The Norwegian government was outraged. Foreign Minister Thorbjoern Jagland called the Australian government's response 'unacceptable and inhumane', and declared that Norway would be reporting Australia to the United Nations maritime agency, refugee agency and the

International Committee of the Red Cross for breaching international maritime and human rights laws.

John Howard rode to electoral victory largely on the back of the dramas unfolding offshore, as the Labor Opposition looked on weakly and ineffectually from the sidelines. Like Parkes, Howard used border politics to promote his image as a political strongman, prepared to risk getting his hands dirty in the defence of the nation's sovereignty. You could hear the echo of Parkes in Howard's statement that 'it is in the national interest that we have the power to prevent, beyond any argument, people infringing the sovereignty of this country'.[10]

His comments touched a deep chord in the Australian psyche. Aversion to newcomers is a familiar national trait. 'It's either "blow them up" or "sink them",' a Queensland publican said of his patrons' response to the scenes of boat people at sea on the television screen in the pub. 'They should be shot and returned home,' Grace Lynch, an elderly piano teacher from Longman in Queensland, declared.[11] Senator Ross Lightfoot from Western Australia revived 'yellow peril' rhetoric in a letter he wrote to *The Australian*, in which he claimed that boat people were criminals and brought disease, and that they 'threaten the peace of mind and sense of security of many Australians, by way of their divergent lifestyle, culture, outlook and values'.[12] A senior Defence analyst agreed, writing that 'illegals may find it difficult to adapt ... [and] may continue with their own cultural/ political practices which may be inappropriate in Australia and may pose concern in terms of local security and ethnic tension'.[13]

Howard, it seems, had played an adroit hand. As history had already shown in the case of the *Afghan* over a century before, turning away outsiders was guaranteed to engender mass support.

—

If the White Australia policy was the political birthmark of Australian nationhood in 1901, then it was a White Ocean policy that dominated the politics of the border a hundred years later. The stage had already been set, two years previously, when a review set up to investigate coastal surveillance led to a massive boost in the funds devoted to strengthening Australia's border control armada. Australia's northern seas became the most heavily policed sections of the national fence. But building or buying more warships for northern waters was only one component of the new strategy. As early as 1999 the government had announced that to rely on a 'Fortress Australia' approach alone was illusory.[14] The key to border protection lay not just in defending one's own territory. Instead, Australia had to *cross* the border in order to carry out defence operations *on the other side*. It was, by the government's own admission, Fortress Australia and Forward Defence in one package.

The Australian Defence Force (ADF) was given un-precedented and far-reaching powers to ensure asylum seekers on boats did not ever reach Australian territory. The full impli-cations of their tactics are still coming to light. One manifes-tation of the new approach involved a 'disruption' campaign in Indonesia aimed at stopping refugees embarking for Australia. Disruption strategies included 'interfering' with refugee boats, and there are indications, not yet substantiated, that these acts of interference in some cases proved fatal to the people who boarded them. Australian and Indonesian police were en-couraged to cooperate in preventing passengers from either getting to the boat's departure point, arresting the organisers or, in the words of the Commissioner of the Australian Federal Police, 'in other ways to disrupt the gathering of the people prior to the vessel departing'.[15] Border politics, it seems, no longer had borders.

—

The *Tampa* affair was the catalyst for an aggressive new regime in Australia's northern waters. Code-named Operation Relex, it was launched in the seas between Christmas Island and Ashmore Reef. 'Was this a new style of operation for the Navy? The answer is yes,' Vice Admiral David Shackleton remarked subsequently. 'We had not done this type of operation before.'[16]

The main aim of Operation Relex was to prevent asylum seekers getting to Australian waters. It was imagined, in Defence Speak, as a 'forward deterrence strategy' and included a directive to escort, tow or turn vessels around and send them back to Indonesia, a marked shift from previous operations that sought to detect and intercept boats inside Australian waters and escort them to Australian ports.

Operation Relex resembled a process of war. Aside from the 25 Navy vessels already on patrol from August 2001, there were also three cryptically named 'transit security elements', with 52 soldiers attached to each; Coastwatch patrol craft that were redeployed from Christmas Island in order to support the ADF in the Timor and Arafura Seas; two Air Force P-3 Orions; and Navy helicopters. Backing up all of this as part of John Howard's 'whole of government' approach were an incredible number of senior government agencies. Departments of Defence, DIMIA, the Federal Police (AFP) and Foreign Affairs and Trade (DFAT); Customs, Coastwatch, the Australian Security and Intelligence Organisation (ASIO) and the Offices of National Assessments (ONA) and Strategic Crime Assessments were all directly involved.[17]

Then there was the Illegal Immigration Information

Oversight Committee under the auspices of ONA; the Operational Coordination Committee chaired by DIMIA; and the Joint AFP-DIMIA People Smuggling Strike Team — three new agencies created to collect intelligence relating to refugee movements. Another organisation, the Australian Theatre Joint Intelligence Centre (ASTJIC), ran an intelligence watch 24 hours a day, plus a special team working seven days a week specifically to support Relex operations. I have listed all of the above to demonstrate just how acute the Australian surveillance of its northern borders became.

The war-like posture of Operation Relex was compounded by the secrecy surrounding it. Relex was controlled all the way from the prime minister's office, and the Navy was instructed to seek government advice and approval at every stage of operations at sea. Documents obtained by the *Sydney Morning Herald* in October 2002 show that both John Howard and Minister for Defence Peter Reith tracked confrontations with boats and boarding operations during the election campaign period in late 2001, almost to the hour.[18] Reith retained absolute control over all information relating to Relex activities, and Defence personnel were strictly forbidden to talk outside their own circle.

The implications of all this were revealed most forcefully in what became known as the 'children overboard' affair. During the early afternoon of 6 October, a 20–25 metre wooden boat carrying 223 passengers and crew was intercepted by HMAS *Adelaide*, about 100 nautical miles north of Christmas Island, well outside Australian territory. The boat ignored warnings to turn back, and reached Australian waters in the early hours of 7 October. At this point warning shots were fired into the water in front of the boat. It was a tactic already familiar to traditional Indonesian fishermen, although not to asylum seekers. In the darkness about fourteen people jumped into the water in fright.

Commander Banks was in charge of the *Adelaide*. As he later told a Senate inquiry, at 4.30 a.m. he manoeuvred his ship 'more aggressively close to the vessel to slow it down', and with this distraction, performed an 'assault type non-compliant boarding'. At 4.45 a.m., the vessel's course was altered back towards Indonesia. According to some of the Iraqi refugees on board, the Australian officers who boarded the boat and turned it around pushed the engine speed up too high. At first a heavy smoke filled the boat, and then the engine spluttered and died out completely. 'We couldn't hear the engines any more and there was no more smoke.' The Australian officers left the Indonesian crew 'a small compass, beside it drawing an arrow that leads to the direction of Indonesia'.[19] They were now in international waters, without a functioning engine, water pump or rudder. For two hours the passengers and crew bailed water from the vessel with jugs and buckets, but to little avail. The boat was sinking. Some of them waved a white sheet in a frantic signal of distress.

Meanwhile, that same day, Minister for Immigration Philip Ruddock arrived at a press conference, where he stunned reporters by declaring that, from a boat of mostly Iraqi asylum seekers, 'a number of children have been thrown overboard, again with the intention of putting us under duress . . . I regard this as one of the most disturbing practices I've come across. It was clearly planned and premeditated'.

John Howard went on talkback radio the next day with host Alan Jones: 'Quite frankly Alan, I don't want in this country people who are prepared, if those reports are true, to throw their own children overboard. And that kind of emotional blackmail is very distressing.'

Peter Reith followed: 'It is an absolute fact, children were thrown in the water . . . if you don't accept that, you don't accept anything.'[20] Two days had passed since the federal election had been called.

Throughout all of this, the *Adelaide* was still tracking the boat, and in constant contact with the prime minister's office. After receiving the go-ahead from Canberra, Commander Banks hitched up the unseaworthy boat, turned away from the Timor Sea and started towing it all the way back to Christmas Island. Throughout the next 24 hours, the boat's condition steadily deteriorated. By 4.30 p.m. the next day, 8 October, water was coming in over the freeboard. Naval personnel again boarded the boat and attempted to fix the engine, with no success. A pump brought over from the *Adelaide* proved useless. Still the passengers were kept on the boat. The boarding officer made repeated requests to Commander Banks to move the women and children off the vessel, but his request was refused.[21] Water continued to flood the boat. Women were crying, the men shouting for help, everyone praying for mercy. They were told that the commander of the *Adelaide* was reporting directly to the prime minister's office, and that the answer had to come from him.

When the answer did come, it was frightening. In the words of the Iraqis, they were told that the officers would only come to their rescue 'when your boat is completely submerged and you all must go in the water with your kids and women. Then and only then, our orders will give us the permission for helping you from drowning'.[22] About 5 p.m., the boat started to sink rapidly, and people were taking to the water as the bow went under. They were rescued by Australian officers who jumped in after them. The asylum seekers lost everything but their lives.

Someone took photos. These were sent to a number of Defence email addresses to highlight the bravery of the ADF officers involved in the rescue. 'LSCK Jason "Dogs" Barker shows dogged determination as he helped rescue women and children by dragging them to safety during the rescue' read one caption. 'The big-hearted Leading Seaman also demonstrated Navy's core value of COURAGE' said another. It was these blurry photos that Defence Minister Reith chose to release to the media on 10 October, with the explanatory texts removed, to prove that children were in the water.

Three days had now elapsed since Philip Ruddock made his first comments to the press. The Defence Force released secret statements at the highest levels confirming that no children had been thrown overboard. But Ruddock, Reith and Howard continued to make the claim despite the evidence to the contrary, during an election campaign in which border protection and asylum seekers were prominent issues. A subsequent Senate Inquiry in 2002 found that Peter Reith had deceived the Australian people, but how much the prime minister knew wasn't resolved. This was again under scrutiny as Australia went into the 2004 election. Mike Scrafton, a senior advisor to Reith at the time of the affair, sent an open letter to *The Australian* on 16 August 2004, in which he alleged that on the evening of 7 November 2001 he held three phone conversations with John Howard, alerting the prime minister to the inaccuracy of the 'children overboard' claim. This was in direct conflict with the prime minister's repeated denials that anybody had told him before the federal election of doubts about the story's veracity.

The handling of the *SIEV 4* (SIEV is an acronym for Suspected Illegal Entry Vessel, and 4 indicates the fourth boat to be intercepted during Relex) 'was to be a public show of the Government's strength on the border protection issue, and the behaviour of the unauthorised arrivals a public justification for the policy'.[23] Keeping them on board their sinking vessel right up until the last moment was not a split decision, but an integral part of Relex strategy. An Australian warship is legally part of Australian territory. But by the Navy's own admission, the Safety of Life at Sea (SOLAS) principle, respected and upheld by mariners the world over, was seriously endangered by the Relex approach. It was a profound example of the lengths the government was prepared to go to ensure that asylum seekers would be kept out of Australia.

—

Relex was a brutal and bloody operation. International maritime conventions respected around the world were summarily broken. Boats that could barely float were repeatedly towed back to international waters, rather than escorted to the nearest Australian port of call, often breaking up at sea under the strain. Passengers were detained on leaky boats, even when the boat was sinking. Asylum seekers alleged that they were sometimes sprayed with capsicum spray or threatened with electric batons. Confusion, anger and panic reigned on the boats. Passengers alleged that they were often deceived by Australian officers in their attempts to get boats out of Australian waters. People died.

The *Aceng* was the first boat to face the Relex blockade, bound for Ashmore Reef when it was intercepted by the *Warramunga* on 7 September 2001. Two attempts by Australian officers to board and turn the boat back towards the high seas had failed. Each time, heaving under the weight of the 228 passengers on board — nearly half of them of children, and one heavily pregnant woman — the boat turned back for Ashmore. The third boarding took place at midnight. Women who had barricaded themselves in the wheelhouse 'began crying and screaming hysterically', and as the situation rapidly deteriorated the Australian officers again withdrew, and again the *Aceng* resumed its course for Ashmore. This time it was negotiation that secured the Iraqi passengers' acquiescence.

Reassured that refugee processing would begin the next morning, they allowed themselves to be transferred to the *Manoora*, the Australian heliport that had loaded up with the *Tampa's* Afghan rescuees only four days before, as it passed by the reef on its way to the Pacific. The Iraqis climbed aboard, grateful that their cases for asylum would soon be heard and that the end of their terrible ordeal was finally within sight. 'When we saw the Australian flag on the *Manoora*, we were relieved. We thought the flag will protect us from now on, particularly as we were told by some Australians that the ship will be heading for Darwin.'[24] Kept entirely separate from the Afghans held in the stifling and dark hold below deck, the Iraqis swelled the number of asylum seekers on board to 600.

After a month at sea, they found themselves moored at a tiny, heat-stricken, volcanic island in the Pacific. A hastily constructed camp of tents pitched in the hard ground, surrounded by high wire fences and the Pacific Ocean, awaited them. They had been tricked. This was Nauru, not Darwin. The Iraqis, after standing their ground for days in refusing to leave the ship, were eventually forcibly removed from the *Manoora* by armed Australian officers. They had just become the first involuntary recruits for Australia's 'Pacific Solution'.

In an extreme move to ensure asylum seekers never reached Australia's shores, the Australian government had managed to convince Nauru's prime minister, Rene Harris, to accept them instead. In return, the bankrupt island received millions of dollars. Manus, a small island in Papua New Guinea, became the other offshore detention camp for Australia's asylum seekers. These camps demonstrated just how much farther Australia's borders were now stretching outwards into the Pacific. Over the next four months, 1000 others joined the first group from the *Tampa* and the *Aceng*. The press was muzzled. The asylum seekers quickly, efficiently, sank from public view.

Operation Relex continued until December 2001. Although aggressive tactics at sea were not new, Relex and the Howard border campaign institutionalised a permanent state of wartime in the Timor Sea. It left a bitter and traumatic legacy. Senior RAN officers testified that Relex turned what had once been a civil and cooperative relationship between Australian officers and boat people at sea into tense and desperate confrontations. 'It is certainly fair to say,' ventured Rear Admiral Smith, 'that the change in the behaviour pattern of these people is directly linked to the change in attitude in the Navy, generated by the policy that was implemented.'[25]

Many of those who boarded the boats had already been declared genuine refugees in need of resettlement by the Indonesia-based United Nations High Commission for Refugees. Some were known to have waited in Indonesia for over two years for a response from Australian Immigration authorities. By the time the *SIEV X* sank off the Indonesian coast with the loss of 352 lives, among them at least 30 who had already secured official refugee status, serious questions were being raised in Defence circles about the human and moral cost of such an approach. But the Howard Government called it a success. An election was won, and the numbers of asylum seekers reaching Australian territory by boat dropped. In the wry words of political journalist Mungo MacCallum, without the *Tampa* 'John Howard would have invented it, and to a large extent that is what happened anyway'.[26]

In 1999, two boats of Chinese asylum seekers landed on Australia's east coast — one in Cairns in far north Queensland, the other at Scott's Head in northern New South Wales. It was the place of their arrival that caused gravest offence. Victorian

Premier Jeff Kennett's description of the 'undetected arrival of so many people on our shores just above Sydney Harbour' invoked the image of Sydney Harbour to encourage the idea of people illegally breezing in through Australia's gateway.[27] It was as if they had marched straight in through the front door, rather than snuck in through the back. This was no longer something that only happened 'out there'. Nowhere along Australia's 'unguarded coastline', of which there was 37 000 kilometres, a figure repeated often in the media in the next month, was safe. Coastwatch announced that it was unable to 'keep Australia safe from incursion unless every citizen is prepared to act as the nation's ears and eyes'.[28] Suddenly, the borders were everywhere.

The arrival of the Chinese asylum seekers unleashed a frenzy of predictions about the 'floods', 'epidemics', 'rising tides', 'armadas', 'streams', 'scores', 'pipelines', 'tidal waves' and 'tsunamis' of people and boats massing on Australia's borders. The stormy vocabulary alone was prescriptive. It was as if the ocean itself could no longer be kept separate from the land. It, too, had become part of the threat, propelling unwanted foreigners towards the besieged land with supernatural force, obliterating the nation's borders in its wake.

Australia came to nationhood amid fears of a China popularly imagined as a 'great dam, soon to burst, sending inundating rivers and flows of migrants into neighbouring countries'.[29] The idea of the Chinese as a massive horde gathering on the horizon to swamp Australia found new life in the invasion fears of the late twentieth century. 'The sheer size of the potential flood of undocumented migrants from this [Asian] region is cause for concern,' the director of the Australian Defence College asserted in his discussion paper on people smuggling. 'China alone has an estimated 100 million strong "floating population" who are seeking employment.'[30]

The image of the boat people, once associated with poverty and desperation, underwent a dramatic transformation. They were no longer victims of circumstance but wealthy 'paying passengers', with the means to pay large sums of money to smugglers so that they could 'jump the queue'. The *Daily Telegraph* described the Chinese who landed on the east coast as 'designer boat people'.[31] Immigration Minister Philip Ruddock informed the public in a newspaper interview that 'so-called boat people are flying first class into Indonesia and Malaysia before boarding rickety boats for Australia'.[32] 'Queue-jumper' became a popular synonym for 'asylum seeker', and although more moderate voices spoke out about the absence of queues, let alone Australian embassies, in most places that asylum seekers were fleeing from, they were drowned out in what can only be described as a ritual of denigration.

Within the Australian community, there were those who continued to speak out against the government's harsh stance on asylum seekers and protest against the queue-jumper stereotype. As stories began to filter through about human rights abuses in detention centres and at sea, many people's reactions turned from shock and disbelief to anger. But there was one group that received no sympathy. People smugglers, according to the media, the politicians, the academics, even the asylum seekers themselves, epitomised the most degenerate and immoral examples of the human race, 'scum of the earth', to quote the South Australian premier, John Olsen, who even went on to say they were reason enough for the reintroduction of capital punishment in Australia.[33]

Initially, the people smuggler was imagined as Chinese.

Depravity, disease, sin and crime were traits commonly attributed to the Chinese in the late nineteenth century, and the image of the crafty, immoral gangster had more than superficial resonance over a century later in people-smuggling discourse. 'Wherever there's a Chinatown, there's a people-smuggling racket,' one university lecturer from Queensland informed the media in 1999.[34] Mafia references were invoked. The *Sydney Morning Herald* detailed how the Chinese smugglers were 'controlled by an "international mafia" — a cartel of criminals, career racketeers and corrupt . . . officials for whom money is no object'.[35]

In another article, *The Australian* described how the 'outbound traffic in human cargo has been gathering strength and voracity, run by powerful criminals known locally as "snakeheads", with links to Triads that dominate the world's Chinatowns'.[36] Australians were learning to see themselves as the victims of a premeditated attack. By the time of the *Tampa* affair in 2001, Arabs had begun to replace the Asians in the smuggling trade, and were also making up the bulk of the passengers on the boats. The plane attacks on the Twin Towers in New York on September 11, 2001 led to more sinister allegations, and the new image of the smuggler/ asylum seeker as an Arab cemented their montrosity. Senior politicians warning that there were in all likelihood terrorists lurking among them. 'REVEALED AMONG THE BOAT PEOPLE: MASS MURDERERS' screamed one headline. Underneath, the article quoted Philip Ruddock as saying that 'at least one in 10 illegal immigrants would be of interest to anti-terrorist authorities'.[37]

It is not certain where Ruddock got this information, which later turned out to be unsubstantiated. But two days before the 2001 federal election, John Howard was still embellishing the theme: 'There is a possibility some people having links with organisations that we don't want in this country might use the path of an asylum seeker in order to get here.'[38] There were, of course, many who found the idea that a terrorist would choose a rickety wooden boat, in all likelihood to be turned back at sea, or to spend months or years in an isolated outback detention centre while their entire life history was investigated, suspect. But the idea that the Arabs, like the Chinese before them, were unscrupulously abusing the sympathies of an unsuspecting Australian public stuck.

It was the Indonesian crews, made up of poor fishermen and farmers, who paid the price for the crime of people-smuggling, not the organisers of these operations. The Rotenese fishermen were among the first to be approached by organisers looking to transport refugees to Ashmore Reef, and Pepela was regularly visited in the search for boats and crews. Community resistance in Pepela to the trade was apparently strong, though Sadli told me that he could sympathise with those fishermen who saw the work as an opportunity to pay off their debts, and who believed this was 'better than being caught for fishing and being jailed again which created more debts'. He himself was opposed to it on ethical grounds. Others feared endangering what little fishing access Rotenese fishermen still had to Australian waters.

With offers of substantial financial rewards for the short trip to Ashmore Reef, some Rotenese fishermen did accept the offer. It comes as little surprise that marginalised sailors with such limited options for exercising their intimate knowledge of these waters would look to other ways of utilising their skills for survival.[39] Their fishing operations, as we have seen, were always commercial, and catered to the demands of the Asian market. In a sense, the shift to people ferrying among some Rotenese fishermen was another form of adaptation to new market forces. Unable to operate within a traditional framework of survival, forbidden to modernise or to participate in the industrialised world, trapped by unworkable regulations and powerless to change them, Indonesian fishermen started to live up to the myth of itinerancy foisted on to them for decades.

For the asylum seekers, the Indonesian crews were the last link in a long, arduous journey. After paying between $5000 and $10 000, those fleeing Afghanistan or Iraq generally flew into Malaysia or Jakarta, where organisers or middlemen arranged their transport to an eastern Indonesian port.[40] Rote, Java, Bali, Lombok, Flores, Alor and Bima were common departure points for boats to Ashmore Reef and Christmas Island. Fishermen were offered sums of, on average, $200, although I have spoken to men who were given as little as $60. Those who queried the low pay were told to 'take it or leave it'. Many were promised larger sums once the job was done, but invariably these were not forthcoming. Others got nothing at all. Often pay was collectable only on completion of the job, which meant that those who went to jail missed out. Others returned home to find the organisers had disappeared, never to be seen again.[41]

History has demonstrated that building a higher fence does not stop people fleeing war, persecution or poverty, it merely forces them to take higher risks in their pursuit of safety. A more aggressive maritime environment contributed to the shift in the nature of people-smuggling operations. What were once small-scale, amateurish and overt operations became increasingly large-scale, covert enterprises involving a more criminal element and high-level official corruption.[42] As the operations got larger and the boats bigger and less seaworthy, the make-up of the crews changed too. Often they included only one or two experienced seamen, with the rest made up of young men or boys who had never even been to sea before, to cook or bale water. Juveniles were increasingly in demand by the Indonesia-based operators, who knew they would be dealt with more leniently by the Australian criminal justice system. As penalties for people smuggling increased, the operators also encouraged a 'dump and depart' method of transportation, instructing the Indonesian crews to unload passengers on the first available piece of land, usually Ashmore Reef, before quickly withdrawing from Australian waters.[43]

Often the asylum-seekers, trapped on boats that started to break apart at sea, or turned back from Australian waters, exhausted and desperate, blamed the Indonesian crews, threatening them with violence if they didn't get them to their destination. Indonesian skippers repeatedly told Australian boarding parties that they feared their throats would be cut if the boats were turned around.[44] Ted Wilkinson, the Broome Legal Aid lawyer often called upon to represent the crews in court, believes his clients were as much in the dark as their paying passengers, just as ignorant of the fate that awaited them and just as frightened. Most of the men he represented on people-smuggling charges were uneducated and impoverished, with no appreciation of the consequences of their actions:

> Everything's organised for them. They're just basically the conduits to take these people to Australia, and they really don't understand what they're getting themselves into . . . And I doubt once even these people have been sentenced, whether it will make any kind of ripple in Indonesia at all.[45]

Since the introduction of the *Border Protection (Validation and Enforcement Powers) Act 2001*, these men face a minimum jail term of five years (minimum eight years for a second offence), and a maximum of twenty years. These penalties were designed to 'send a clear message' to Indonesians, but the message was clearly not getting through. Another Perth lawyer, Geoff Vickerage, who represented a 28-year-old fisherman who was sentenced to seven years' jail for people-smuggling, said:

> What they are told, bearing in mind they're generally illiterate fishermen . . . they will come down here, they will be arrested. They'll be put in jail for four months. They'll earn lots of money while they're in jail, and then they'll be flown back to Indonesia. The sum total what they were said to be paid was going to be about $1200.[46]

In Western Australia, those charged with people-smuggling offences are given Legal Aid representation in the courtroom. This is very different to fishing offences, for which defendants receive no automatic legal assistance. The reason for this is that people-smuggling is prosecuted under federal law, and the Legal Aid lawyers acting in these cases are funded by the Commonwealth, while fishing offences are still dealt with under state law. The fact that those who ferried asylum seekers to Australian waters, thus deliberately breaking Australian law, were given free legal advice, while traditional fishermen were denied the same sort of assistance, irks fishermen like Gani Pello. 'Why do [those who escort] illegal immigrants already have lawyers prepared to help them in court?' he asked. 'Do they also pay for their lawyers too? Do they look for their own lawyer? No. The Immigration Department helps them to find a lawyer. How about the traditional fishermen?'

Another discrepancy is that the amount of time crew members charged with people smuggling spend in detention prior to a hearing is counted towards the length of their prison sentence. Because the penalty for illegal fishing is a fine, not a direct prison sentence (they go to jail to repay the fine at a set rate per day), the fishermen are not entitled to count the period in detention before their hearing towards their prison term. These weeks and sometimes months spent out at Willie Creek or in Darwin Harbour are substantial punishment in themselves. Overall, there is a strong belief among the traditional fishermen of Rote that they are punished more severely by the courts than are the people smugglers, in addition to which they incur heavy debts through loss of boats and equipment.

Government officials are not unaware that the people in jail for people smuggling are generally poor fishermen and farmers, rather than master criminals. In 2000, the *Sydney Morning Herald* reported that an AusAID working party had gone to West Timor to investigate the option of aid for the fishermen, including the setting up of fish farms and new methods to improve their catch. A spokesman for Immigration Minister Ruddock told the newspaper that if 'we can increase their level of income from local sustainable fishing we reduce the attractiveness of taking money from the people smugglers'.[47] It was the first and only time that public recognition like this was given by a senior government official. Nevertheless, at the time Rote had never received foreign aid of this kind, despite its being the poorest region in Indonesia. This may be changing. There is now an AusAID project researching the viability of seaweed farming on the island, but how advanced the proposal is remains unclear.

By the time the *Tampa* hit the headlines, there were over 230 Indonesians being held in Australian jails, most of them on charges of people smuggling. Many of them were fishermen by trade. A year later, a minor flurry of publicity surrounding the sentencing of two Indonesian fishermen appeared as a small footnote to the *Tampa* affair. Norbames Nurdin and Bastian Disun were sentenced for bringing the largest numbers of unauthorised arrivals to Australia on board the *Palapa*, and given jail sentences of four and seven years respectively. One of the lawyers involved in the case questioned the apparent reluctance to arrest the people actually responsible for organising the *Palapa* operation. The information provided to federal police by the passengers of the *Tampa* about the organisers was extensive: 'They knew what these organisers looked like, and in some cases, knew where they worked and where they lived . . . From all we can tell, all the efforts of the prosecuting authorities have been to prosecute poor fishermen. None of the organisers involved in the *Tampa* affair have been charged.'[48]

This seems to have been the general trend. The high-profile arrest of one man, Abu Quassey, alleged to have been the main organiser of the vessel in which 352 people drowned, resulted in a six-month jail sentence in Indonesia, before he was sent back to stand trial in Egypt, leading to rumours that Indonesian and Australian police were too much involved to risk exposure by trying the organisers closer to home. It is Indonesian fishermen who have borne the brunt of Australia's harsh border protection laws. There have been record numbers of apprehensions and arrests in the past few years. And now that the asylum seekers have largely disappeared from the northern seascape, the presence of Indonesian fishermen assists in maintaining a sense of emergency and crisis in the region. They are still a concrete target.

It has been said that the land, our country, wherever or whatever that may be, is the place where our dreams materialise.[49] Is this sea the place where our fears materialise?

Like the crowds who lined the docks of Sydney Harbour to fling obscenities at the passengers on board the *Afghan*, the nation has figuratively lined up along the shores of the Timor Sea, flinging the best sticks and stones it could find into its midst. Too many have found their mark.

EPILOGUE

In April 2004, Johni Fakie went to sea for the last time. A big storm struck the small *perahu* he was sailing in with five others. It raged all night. By its end, all that was left of Johni's boat were a few bits of blue timber and torn shreds of sail bobbing about on the ocean's surface. Six boats went down that night. None of the 43 fishermen survived. They didn't stand a chance.

Johni was 28 years old. Rarely seen without his battered guitar in Pepela, he was often surrounded by other young men, singing and strumming old rock songs. He is a dreamer, people in the village would say. Johni was restless for something different. 'There's nothing positive for traditional fishermen,' Johni said on one occasion. He had come to dread going fishing, because of the risk of storms and arrest. Being in jail in Australia had almost driven him mad with worry about his mother and four siblings left behind. In one letter I received from him, he asked how much it cost the Australian people to capture and jail them: 'What if the money was used to sponsor our island so that we could be provided with some basic tools to open up other opportunities . . . so that we would not have to sail again (or return to Australia)? Farming has to be better than this.'[1]

Perhaps the villagers were right to call him a dreamer. But Johni was also a thinker. Over the years that I came to know him, he wrote many long, thoughtful letters about how he viewed the deteriorating situation of his community and his ideas for change. He could never understand why the fishermen were jailed for so long, nor the animosity of the Australian government towards them. His letters were a plea for understanding, a constant attempt to make the Rotenese voice heard. And each one ended as politely, and as hopefully, as it began: 'Firstly we, the Indonesian fishermen, express our deep gratitude for your attention . . . We therefore ask the Australian people and government to help and bring attention to the plight of traditional Indonesian fishermen.'[2]

The Rotenese fishermen have never really surrendered their sovereignty of the Timor Sea, but they do not experience it as the place it once was. Even though they argue that there are no lines in the sea, their journeys are marked by an acute consciousness of them. Along with a certain loss of freedom of movement in these waters comes the loss of other things: the knowledge associated with traditional boat building, as boats are no longer being made to last; pride in their work; the loss of a myriad skills that go with a sustainable traditional industry. Family trips to Ashmore Reef to show their children the 'garden in the sea' are now only a memory. A situation of illegality appears to have become an inevitability. Some say that getting arrested has become a rite of passage for young men. Even the way they now refer to themselves as 'tradition-al' fishermen is a clear appropriation of Australian terminology. There was no need to distinguish themselves as such in the past.

Johni was not alone in his ambivalence and trepidation about life as a fisherman. Older Rotenese fishermen report a reluctance to pass on stories and knowledge about their sea traditions. Sadli said that he has stopped telling the story of Pulau Pasir and the stone fences to the younger generations because he 'didn't see the point anymore'.[3] Often he feels hopeless. 'I haven't yet gone to sea because my wife and children are scared I might be arrested and jailed. Sometimes I think that perhaps I'm one of those people who fail to take responsibility for their family and the future of my children', he wrote, in reference to the debts that will burden him till he dies.[4] Others talk of not wanting their sons to become fishermen. Djishard Bakuama, a fourth-generation fisherman, said that this was an impossible decision: 'Even if I don't teach [my sons], they are living in a fishing environment so that is what they will automatically pick up.'

But neither is Johni alone in thinking about solutions to their current plight. Sadli took a trip the year before Johni died. He travelled to Jakarta, the big city, the centre of gov-ernment — thousands of kilometres from the village of Pepela. Except for his nightmarish stay in Denpasar after he was re-patriated back to Indonesia by Australian immigration auth-orities a few years before, he had never been to a city like this. Sadli carried with him *Troubled Waters* — the documentary film made about the Rotenese fishermen's experience of Australian maritime expansion — and a determination to make himself heard on behalf of the fishermen of Rote. Sadli managed to get access to one official who watched it and was 'very sad', giving him hope that there would be more done about their current desperate plight. He tried to give it to the state television network. In the end, though, it was as he had feared. Indonesia cared little. 'What can I say? People who have a decent income, their ears and their eyes take in our poverty, our tears . . . as if it was a fascinating musical performance.'[5]

We are not used to seeing the sea as a colonial space. Unlike on land, there are no ruins or battle scars or human traces to remind us of the battles of conquest that have gone there before. To a Westerner's eye, the sea is a blank space on the map. This is one of the great myths of Australia's maritime expansion — that the sea was empty and no one suffered from the loss of it.

These are troubled waters. They have a bloody history. Sadli has a message for the Australian government and the Australian people: 'Even though we differ by the colour of skin, our ethnicity and our economic levels, we are still all human beings. Please don't make laws that hurt us fishermen. Because the only reason we go there is to go fishing. No other reason.' His request is simple. He asks for 'better understanding'.[6] It remains to be seen whether his voice will be heard.

NOTES

Introduction

1 There are two contemporary spellings of Rote. Present-day official documents that originate from the central government of Indonesia tend to use 'Roti', while official documents coming from the island itself use 'Rote'. Likewise, the fishing village of Pepela has two common spelling forms, 'Pepela', which the fishermen mostly use, and 'Papela'. In both cases, I have chosen to use the local spelling. However, I acknowledge Professor James Fox's usage of 'Roti', which is the format widely used in world atlases and more widely accepted.

2 Interview (Balint) with Abdul Gani Pello, Pepela, Rote, May 2001.

3 *Troubled Waters*, Resonance Productions, 2001.

4 Christina Stead, *For Love Alone*, Angus & Robertson, Australia, 1966 (first published 1945), p. 1.

5 Arthur Upfield, *Bony and the White Savage*, Sydney, 1987, quoted in Robin Gerster, *Hotel Asia: An Anthology of Australian Literary Travelling to the 'East'*, Penguin Books, Sydney, 1995, p. 6.

6 Anthony J. Brown, *Ill-Starred Captains: Flinders and Baudin*, revised edition, Fremantle Arts Centre Press, 2004, p. 151.

7 Matthew Flinders, *A Voyage to Terra Australis . . . in the Years 1801, 1802 and 1803 in His Majesty's Ship the Investigator*, G. & W. Nicol, London, 1814, p. 172.

8 Ibid, pp. 228–33.

9 Brown, op. cit., p. 364.

10 The term 'Macassan' was used by Campbell MacKnight to describe the crews of the boats that came to north Australia in his book, *The Voyage to Marege: Macassan Trepangers in Northern Australia*, Melbourne University Press, 1976. However, the term is a bit misleading, in that the people crewing were from a number of different ethnic sailing groups of eastern Indonesia.

11 Ian Crawford, *We Won the Victory: Aborigines and Outsiders on the North-West Coast of the Kimberley*, Fremantle Arts Centre Press, Fremantle, 2001, p. 76.

12 Interview (Balint) with Irene and Eric Hunter, One Arm Point Aboriginal Community, 20 April 2001.

The Timor Connection

1 Evidence of pottery found at Groote Eylandt is presumably from Indonesia, and is thought to be 1000 years old. See: David Bulbeck and Barbara Rowley, 'Macassans and their pots in northern Australia', in Clayton Frederickson and Ian Walters (eds), *Altered States: Material Culture Transformations in the Arafura Region*, Northern Territory University Press, Darwin, 2001, p. 55. Anne Clarke cites three pieces of archaeological evidence of Macassan contact dating back 800 years. See: Anne Clarke, 'The "Moorman's Trowsers": Macassan and Aboriginal interactions', in Sue O'Connor and Peter Veth (eds), *East of Wallace's Line: Studies of Past and Present Maritime Cultures of the Indo-Pacific Region*, A. A. Balkema, Rotterdam, The Netherlands, 2000, pp. 325–8.

2 Interview (Balint) with Vanessa Poelina, Broome, 21 February 2001.

3 John Crawford, *History of the Indian Archipelago* (1820), Frank Cass & Co, London, 1967, pp. 441–2.

4 Ibid., p. 441.

5 Alfred R. Wallace, *The Malay Archipelago: The Land of the Orang-Utan and the Birds of Paradise: A Narrative of Travel with Studies of Man and Nature* (1869, MacMillan & Co.), Oxford University Press, 1986, vol. II, p. 158.

6 Ian Crawford, *We Won the Victory: Aborigines and Outsiders on the North-West Coast of the Kimberley*, Fremantle Arts Centre Press, Fremantle, 2001, pp. 70–1.

7 Ibid., p. 71.

8 Campbell C. MacKnight, *The Voyage to Marege: Macassan Trepangers in Northern Australia*, Melbourne University Press, Carlton, 1976, p. 99.

9 Ibid., pp. 78–9.

10 Nonie Sharp, *Saltwater People: The Waves of Memory*, Allen & Unwin, Sydney, 2002, pp. 66–7.

11 George Windsor Earl, 'On the Aboriginal Tribes of the Northern Coast of Australia', *Journal of the Royal Geographic Society*, no. 16, 1846. See also: George Windsor Earl, *Enterprise in Tropical Australia*, Madden & Malcolm, London, 1846.

12 MacKnight (1976), op. cit., p. 85.

13 Ibid., pp. 85–6.

14 Heather Sutherland, 'Eastern Emporium and Company Town: Trade and society in eighteenth century Makassar', in Frank Broeze (ed.), *Brides of the Sea: Port Cities of Asia from the 16th–20th Centuries*, New South Wales University Press, Sydney, 1989, pp. 101–4.

15 Frank Broeze, *Island Nation: A History of Australians and the Sea*, Allen & Unwin, Sydney, 1998, p. 14.

16 George W. Earl, *Sailing Directions for the Arafura Sea*, Hydrographic Office, London and Sydney, 1839, p. 14.

17 Warwick Anderson, *The Cultivation of Whiteness: Science, Health and Racial Destiny in Australia*, Melbourne University Press, Melbourne, 2002, p. 76.

18 'North Coast of New Holland: Dr Wilson's Work', *The Perth Gazette and Western Australian Journal*, 10 December 1836, p. 814.

19 Warwick Anderson, op. cit., p. 77.

20 The presence of earlier non-trepanging Indonesian sites along the Kimberley coast suggests the possibility of an earlier trade in northern Australian products such as tortoiseshell, sandalwood and pearlshell. See: M. J. Morwood and D. R. Hobbs, 'The Asian Connection: Preliminary report on Indonesian trepang sites on the Kimberley coast, N.W. Australia', *Archaeology in Oceania*, no. 32, 1997, pp. 197–206.

21 Interview (Balint) with Eric and Irene Hunter, One Arm Point Aboriginal Community, Dampier Peninsula, 20 April 2001.

22 Quoted in Kristin Joyce and Shellei Addison, *Pearls: Ornament and Obsession*, Thames & Hudson, London, 1992, p. 75.

23 *Inquirer*, 28 April 1875, reprinted in Mike McCarthy, 'Before Broome', *Journal of the Australian Association for Maritime History*, vol. 16, no. 2, 1994, p. 81.

24 Edwin Streeter, *Pearls and Pearling Life*, 1861. Reprinted in John Bailey, *The White Divers of Broome: The True Story of a Fatal Experiment*, Pan Macmillan, Sydney, 2001, p. 23.

25 *The West Australian*, 6 August 1910.

26 Mary Albertus Bain, *Full Fathom Five*, Artlook Books, Perth, 1982, p. 242.

27 Frank Broeze, 'Introduction: Brides of the sea', in F. Broeze (ed.), op. cit., p. 3.

28 *Broome Chronicle*, 13 March 1.

29 Ibid.

30 A. Banjo Paterson, 'The Pearl Diver', *The Collected Verse of A. B. Paterson*, Angus & Robertson Publishers, Sydney (first published 1921), 1986, p. 107.

31 David Day, *Smugglers and Sailors: The Customs History of Australia 1788–1901*, Australian Government Publishing Service, Canberra, 1992, p. 358.

32 Natasha Stacey, 'Boats to Burn: Bajo fishing activity in the Australian Fishing Zone', unpublished PhD thesis, Northern Territory University, 1999, pp. 115–6.

33 Ibid., pp. 111–2.

34 Interview (Balint) with Georgina Kaissis, Broome, 18 July 2000.

35 Interview (Balint) with Mick Manolis, Broome, 20 July 2000.

See also: Komei Hosokawa, 'Malay talk on boat: An account of Broome Pearling Lugger Pidgin', in Donald C. Laycock and Werner Winter (eds), *A World of Language: Papers Presented to Professor S. A. Wurm on his 65th Birthday*, Pacific Linguistics, C-100, 1987, p. 287.

36 Interview (Balint) with Sherena Bin-Hitam, Broome, 19 July 2000.

37 For an overall account of the Broome riots, see: Michael Shaper, 'The Broome race riots of 1920', and Christine Choo, 'Asian men on the West Kimberley coast, 1900–1940', both in Jan Gothard (ed.), *Asian Orientations: Studies in Western Australian History*, no. 16, Centre for Western Australian History, University of Western Australia, 1995.

38 Interview (Balint) with Peter Matsumoto, Broome, 21 July 2000.

39 Bailey, op. cit., p. 292.

Staking the Timor Sea

1 Cited in Anthony Burke, *In Fear of Security: Australia's Invasion Anxiety*, Pluto Press, Sydney, 2001, p. 17.

2 Alison Bashford, 'Quarantine and the imagining of the Australian nation', in *Health: An Interdisciplinary Journal for the Social Study of Health, Illness and Medicine*, vol. 2, no. 4, October 1998.

3 Ibid., p. 394.

4 Cited in Bruce Campbell and Bu Wilson, *The Politics of Exclusion: Indonesian Fishing in the Australian Fishing Zone*, Indian Ocean Centre for Peace Studies Monograph No. 5, Indian Ocean Centre for Peace Studies, Perth WA, 1993, p. 45.

5 Ibid.

6 Letter to the editor, *The Australian*, 24 November 1999.

7 Cited in Ian Davidson, *The Idea of Japan: Western Images, Western Myths*, Secker & Warburg, London, 1996, p. 6.

8 Cited in Jan Wilton and Richard Bosworth, *Old Worlds and New Australia: The Post-war Migrant Experience*, Penguin Books, Ringwood, 1984, p. 4.

9 Department of the North West, *The North and North-West of Western Australia: Its Wealth and Opportunities*, Booklet No. 4, June 1924, p. 3.

10 Cited in Burke, op. cit., p. 16.

11 C. H. Kirmess, *The Australian Crisis*, George Robertson, Melbourne, 1909, p. 335.

12 Griffith Taylor, *Environment, Race and Migration: Fundamentals of Human Distribution: With Special Sections on Racial Classification; and Settlement in Canada and Australia*, University of Toronto Press, Toronto, 1937, p. 394.

13 Cited in Raymond Evans, 'Keep White the Strain: Race relations in a colonial setting', in R. Evans, Kay Saunders, Kathryn Cronin (eds), *Race Relations in Colonial Queensland: A History of Exclusion, Exploitation and Extermination (1975)*, University of Queensland Press, 1993, p. 8.

14 Donald Denoon, 'Temperate medicine and settler capitalism: On the reception of western medical ideas', in Roy Macleod and Milton Lewis (eds), *Disease, Medicine and Empire: Perspectives on Western Medicine and the Experience of European Expansion*, Routledge, London and New York, 1988, p. 125.

15 William Blackstone, *Commentaries on the Laws of England*, vol. 2, Clarendon Press, Oxford, 1979, p. 18.

16 See Nonie Sharp, *Saltwater People: The Waves of Memory*, Allen & Unwin, Sydney, 2002, pp. 152–4.

17 Hugo Grotius, *The Freedom of the Seas or the Right Which Belongs to the Dutch to Take Part in the East Indian Trade*, New York, Orno Press, 1972 [first Latin edition 1633. Ruan Deman Magoffin Translation, *Mare Liberum*], p. 38.

18 John Selden, *Mare Clausum: The Right and Dominion of the Sea* (2 vols), Andrew Kembe and Edward Thomas, London, 1663 [first published by Bonaventura and Abraham Elzevier in Leyden, The Netherlands, 1636].

19 Bonnie McCay, 'Sea tenure and the culture of the commoners' in John Cordell (ed.), *A Sea of Small Boats*, Cultural Survival Report 26, Cultural Survival Inc., Cambridge, 1989, p. 215.

20 R. E. Johannes, 'Traditional marine conservation methods in Oceania and their demise', *Annual Review of Ecological Systems*, no. 9, 1978, pp. 358–9.

21 *The Commonwealth v. Yarmirr; Yarmirr v. Northern Territory (2001)*, *High Court of Australia* 56, 11 October, 2001. See Sharp, op. cit., pp. 9–10.

22 Cited in Maxine Chi, 'Saltwater People: Aboriginal use of sea resources, Broome, Western Australia', unpublished MA thesis, Centre for Aboriginal Studies, Curtin University of Technology, 2002, p. 36.

23 Geoffrey McKee, 'The new Timor Gap: Will Australia now break with the past?' *Inside Indonesia*, vol. 62, April–June 2000.

24 Recent declassified records together with new research has exposed the level of Australian political complicity in the invasion and subsequent genocide of East Timorese people. On this subject, see: Rodney Tiffen, *Diplomatic Deceits: Government, Media and East Timor*, University of NSW Press, Sydney, 2001; James Dunn, *Timor: A People Betrayed*, ABC Books, Sydney, 1996 (first published 1983); Don Greenlees and Robert Garran, *Deliverance: The Inside Story of East Timor's Fight for Freedom*, Allen & Unwin, Sydney, 2002.

25 Burke, op. cit., pp. 150–1.

26 'PM defends "fair" deal for Timor', *Sydney Morning Herald*, 20 May 2002.

27 'Timor gas billions all at sea', *Sydney Morning Herald*, 27 March 2002. Also: 'Changes to International Dispute Resolution', Press Statement issued by the Attorney General's Department and the Department of Foreign Affairs and Trade, Parliament House, Canberra, 25 March 2002.

28 'Downer rules border changes out of bounds', *The Weekend Australian*, 25 May 2002.

29 Cited in Frank Brennan SJ, 'The Timor Sea's oil and gas: What's fair?', *Catholic Social Justice Series*, no. 51, 2004, p. 43.

30 Joseph Conrad, *An Outcast of the Islands*, Oxford University Press, Oxford and New York, 2002 (first published 1892), p. 14.

31 Interview (Balint) for *Troubled Waters*, Resonance Productions, 2001.

Of Fish and Men

1 *Troubled Waters*, Resonance Productions, 2001.

2 James J. Fox, *Harvest of the Palm: Ecological Change in Eastern Indonesia*, Harvard University Press, Cambridge and London, 1977, p. 28.

3 Ibid., pp. 24–30.

4 Adrian Horridge, *The Prahu*, Oxford University Press, London, 1981, p. 66.

5 Michael Southon, *The Navel of the* Perahu*: Meaning and Values in the Maritime Trading Economy of a Butonese Village*, Research School of Pacific and Asian Studies, The Australian National University, Canberra, 1995, pp. 93–8.

6 Ibid., pp. 106–7.

7 Letter to the author from Rocky Martimus (originally of Oelaba, Rote), from Broome Regional Prison, March 1998.

8 Southon, op. cit., p. 105.

9 Natasha Stacey, 'Boats to Burn: Bajo Fishing Activity in the Australian Fishing Zone', unpublished PhD thesis, Northern Territory University, 1999, pp. 103–5.

10 Ibid., p. 82.

11 Statistics supplied by Tom Therik, University Kristas, Kupang, Nusa Tengarra, Indonesia, August 2001.

12 Letter to the author from Yusuf Messak (origin given as Rote), from Broome Regional Prison, March 1998.

13 G. Marcus and M. Fischer, *Anthropology as Cultural Critique: An Experimental Moment in the Human Sciences*, University of Chicago Press, 1986, p. 78.

14 Stacey, op. cit., pp. 65–6.

15 Nick Burmingham, 'Unwelcome visitors at the two hundredth birthday party: A perspective on recent illegal Indonesian fishing in Australian waters', *Northern Perspective*, vol. II, no. 1, 1989, p. 4.

16 John Darling (writer/director), *Below the Wind*, Ronin Films, Canberra, 1994 (screened on ABC Television, 1995).

17 Stacey, op. cit., p. 66.

18 Bruce C. Campbell and Bu V. Wilson, *The Politics of Exclusion: Indonesian Fishing in the Australian Fishing Zone*, Indian Ocean Centre for Peace Studies, no. 5, 1993, p. 97.

19 Interview (Balint) with Agung Prasata and Gani Pello together, Pepela, Rote, May 2001.

20 Stacey, op. cit., p. 251.

21 Ibid., pp. 249–50.

22 Interview (Balint) with Peter Isak Husein, Pepela, Rote, May 2001.

23 Interview (Balint) with Sadli Hudari Ardani, op. cit.

Mare Nullius

1 D. L. Serventy, 'Indonesian fishing activity in Australian waters', *Australian Geographer*, vol. I, no. 1, 1952, p. 13.

2 Cited in Natasha Stacey, 'Boats to Burn: Bajo Fishing Activity in the Australian Fishing Zone', unpublished PhD thesis, Northern Territory University, 1999, p. 136. From the original CSIRO Biological Log of the FRV *Warreen*, Cruise Number 35, July to November 1949. Unpublished.

3 Serventy, op. cit.

4 In 1968, the Act was replaced by the *Continental Shelf (Living Natural Resources) Act*.

5 Cited in Bruce Campbell and Bu Wilson, *The Politics of Exclusion: Indonesian Fishing in the Australian Fishing Zone*, Indian Ocean Centre for Peace Studies, no. 5, 1993, p. 26.

6 Ibid., p. 36.

7 For both quotes, see ibid.

8 Henry Reynolds, *The Law of the Land*, Penguin Books, Ringwood, 1987, p. 32.

9 Cited in Henry Reynolds, *Dispossession*, Allen & Unwin, Sydney, 1989, p. 72.

10 Cited in Campbell and Wilson, ibid., p. 36.

11 Department of Foreign Affairs and Trade (DFAT), 'The Control of Indonesian Traditional Fishing in the Australian Fishing Zone of North-West Australia', unpublished report, Department of Foreign Affairs and Trade, Canberra, 1998, p. 1.

12 R. Gerard Ward, *Widening Worlds, Shrinking Worlds? The Reshaping of Oceania*, Centre for Contemporary Pacific Division of Pacific and Asian History, Research School of Pacific and Asian Studies, Australian National University, Canberra, 1999, pp. 7–8.

13 Greg Dening, 'Songlines and seaways: A reflection on the occasion of the rehanging of the Australian and Pacific Collections in the National Gallery of Australia', in *Performances*, Melbourne University Press, Melbourne, 1996, p. 213.

14 See J. B. Harley, 'Maps, knowledge and power', in D. Cosgrove and S. Daniels (eds), *The Iconography of Landscape*, Cambridge University Press, 1988; J. B. Harley, 'Deconstructing the map', in T. Barnes and J. Duncan (eds), *Writing Worlds: Discourse, Text and Metaphor in the Representation of the Landscape*, Routledge & Kegan Paul, London and New York, 1992. See also Jeremy Black, *Maps and Politics*, University of Chicago Press, Chicago, 1997, p. 22.

15 Interview (Balint) for *Troubled Waters*, Resonance Productions, 2001.

16 *Troubled Waters*, Resonance Productions, 2001.

17 Anthony Reid, 'Illegal Entry! Indonesian Fishermen Detained in Broome: A Report on the Social and Economic Background', Occasional Paper Series No. 1, Centre for Southeast Asian Studies, Northern Territory University, 1992, p. 8.

18 'Statement of facts Indonesian Fishing Vessel *Sirman Jaya*', WA Legal Aid, Broome Office, 16 May 1998. Pers. comm.

19 The Law Reform Commission, *The Recognition of Aboriginal Customary Laws*, Vol. 2, Report No. 31, Australian Publishing Service, Canberra, 1986, p. 121. Also quoted in Campbell and Wilson, op. cit., p. 78.

20 Natasha Stacey, 'Boats to Burn: Bajo Fishing Activity in the Australian Fishing Zone', unpublished PhD thesis, Northern Territory University, 1999, p. 278.

21 Article 10 (3) Torres Strait Treaty (1978).

22 *Troubled Waters*, op. cit.

23 Natasha Stacey, op. cit., p. 281.

24 Marianna Torgovnick, *Gone Primitive: Savage Intellects, Modern Lives*, The University of Chicago Press, Chicago and London, 1990, p. 9.

25 *Fremantle Gazette*, 1 October 1980, p. 7.

26 Interview (Balint) with Abdul Gani Pello, Pepela, Rote, Indonesia, May 2001.

27 *Troubled Waters*, op. cit.

28 Jill Elliott, 'Indonesian Fishermen: A Western Australian Perspective', unpublished paper, Broome, Western Australia, 1998. Courtesy of the Kimberley Indonesia Friendship Association.

29 *Indonesian Observer*, 2 July 1994.

30 Letter from Djishard Bakuama and eight others in Broome Regional Prison, *The West Australian*, 5 April 1998.

Hooks and Sinkers

1 John Darling (writer/director), *Below the Wind*, Ronin Films, Canberra, 1994 (screened ABC Television, 1995).

2 Interview (Balint) for *Troubled Waters*, Resonance Productions, 2001.

3 Interview (Balint), Broome Regional Prison, 14 May 1998.

4 Interview (Balint), Willie Creek Detention Centre, 27 May 1998.

5 Interview (Balint) with Saryono, Musa, Jalating, Dania, Pahang, Marzuki and Djishard Bakuama, Broome, 28 May 1998.

6 David Walker, 'Survivalist anxieties: Australian responses to Asia, 1890s to the present', *Australian Historical Studies*, vol. 33, no. 120, October 2002, p. 329.

7 Ghassan Hage, *Against Paranoid Nationalism: Searching for Hope in a Shrinking Society*, Pluto Press, Sydney, 2003, pp. 31–2.

8 *Troubled Waters*, Resonance Productions, 2001.

9 'Administrative Arrangements for Indonesian Fishermen Detained in Australian Waters', Report Under S35A of the *Ombudsman's Act 1976*, Canberra, August 1998.

10 Interview (Balint) with Senator Ian MacDonald, Parliament House, Canberra, 18 August 2003, for *Insight*, SBS Television.

11 Ruth Balint, 'The Death of Mansur', *Insight*, SBS Television, 21 August 2003.

12 Risman Wabulah's statutory declaration, Folio 8, Coronial file in relation to the death of Mansur La-Ibu, Coronial Inquest into the Death of Mansur, Darwin Coroner's Court, 16–20 February 2004.

13 Colin MacDonald QC, Opening Address, Coronial Inquest into the Death of Mansur, Darwin Coroner's Court, 16 February 2004.

14 Interview (Balint) with Vice Consul A. F. Arif Soepalal SH, Consulate of the Republic of Indonesia, Northern Territory, 23 July 2003.

15 File No. D0021/2003, Finding of Mr Greg Cavenagh, Territory Coroner, Inquest into the Death of Mansur La Ibu [2004] NTMC 020, p. 17.

16 Interview (Balint) for *Troubled Waters*, Resonance Productions, 2001.

17 This is incorporated in the Commonwealth *Maritime Legislation Amendment Act (1994)*, which amends the *Seas and Submerged Lands Act (1973)*.

18 'Submissions with Respect to the Sentencing of Good Behaviour Bonds and Estreatment of Indonesian Nationals Toto and Samah', unpublished, undated manuscript, Broome Legal Aid Office.

19 *La Ode Arafin and Others v. Colin William Ostle and Others*, Full Court of the Supreme Court of Western Australia Library, No 8923AC, 18 June 1991, p. 22.

20 Magistrate Colin Roberts, 'Trial of the *Sirman Jaya*', Broome Court of Petty Sessions, 21 May 1998.

21 Interview (Balint) with Indonesian prisoner, Broome Regional Prison, 13 May 1998.

22 Natasha Stacey, 'Boats To Burn: Bajo Fishing Activity in the Australian Fishing Zone', unpublished PhD thesis, Northern Territory University, 1999, p. 285.

23 *Troubled Waters*, op. cit.

24 James J. Fox, 'Reefs and shoals in Australia-Indonesia relations: Traditional Indonesian fishermen', in Anthony Milner and Mary Quilty (eds), *Australia in Asia: Episodes*, Oxford University Press, Melbourne, 1998, p. 123.

25 Interview (Balint) with La Bau Wajo, La Nunu and La Maana, Broome, 28 May 1998.

26 'Trial of the *Sirman Jaya*', from Maginti, Broome Court of Petty Sessions, 21 May 1998.

27 Interview (Balint) with Johni Fakie, Pepela, Rote, 26 May 2001.

28 *Troubled Waters*, op. cit.

29 *Troubled Waters*, op. cit.

30 Jonathon Hunyor, 'Indonesian Fishermen Before the Australian Courts: That Sinking Feeling', One Day Workshop on Indonesian Fishing in North Australian Waters, unpublished paper, Northern Territory University, Darwin, 9 March 2001.

31 Interview (Balint) with Ted Wilkinson, Broome, 11 May 1998.
32 Stacey, op. cit, pp. 285–6.
33 Fox, op. cit., p. 131.
34 Interview (Balint) for *Troubled Waters*, Resonance Productions, 2001.
35 Stacey, op. cit., p. 105.
36 Interview (Balint) with Pahang, Broome Regional Prison, 29 May 1998.
37 *Troubled Waters*, op. cit.
38 Interview (Balint) with Matteos Tunga's parents, West Timor, May 2001.
39 *Troubled Waters*, op. cit.
40 *West Australian*, 8 January 1991.
41 *West Australian*, 13 September 1988.
42 *Broome Advertiser*, 29 July 1998.
43 The Hon. Philip Ruddock MP, Letter addressed to 'Indonesian Fishermen, Broome Regional Prison', dated 26 May 1998, personal copy.
44 Interview (Balint) with Australian prison officer, Perth Airport, 10 April 2001.
45 Letter to the author from Hanafi Laduma, Pepela, Rote, in Broome Regional Prison, West Australia. Received 10 January 2000. No date.

Stone Fences and Sad Stories

1 Matthew Flinders, *A Voyage to Terra Australis*, vol. II, G. & W. Nicol and Pall Mall Books, London, 1814, pp. 229–33.
2 This story is an amalgamation of two accounts by Sadli, one as told to me in Pepela in May 2001, and one told to Geoff Havel on a visit to Pepela in 1998, 'Brief History of the People of Rote Finding the Sand Island', courtesy of the West Australian Maritime Museum.
3 James J. Fox, 'Reefs and shoals in Australia–Indonesia relations: Traditional Indonesian fishermen', in Anthony Milner and Mary Quilty (eds), *Australia in Asia: Episodes*, Oxford University Press, Melbourne 1998, pp. 118–9.
4 Natasha Stacey, 'Boats to Burn: Bajo Fishing Activity in the

Australian Fishing Zone', unpublished PhD thesis, Northern Territory University, 1999, p. 147.

5 Daniel Dwyer, 'Fishers of people: From reef fishing to refugees. The changing role of Indonesian sailors and their *perahus* at Ashmore Reef, north Australia', in Clayton Frederickson and Ian Walters (eds), *Altered States: Material Culture Transformations in the Arafura Region*, Northern Territory University Press, Darwin, 2001, p. 37. See also: G. Marston, 'Abandonment of territorial claims: The cases of Bouvet and Spratly Islands', *British Year Book of International Law 1986*, Clarendon Press, Oxford, 1987, p. 346.

6 Version as told to Geoff Havel, op. cit.

7 *Troubled Waters*, Resonance Productions, 2001.

8 For a full list of protected species at Ashmore Reef, see: *Ashmore Reef National Nature Reserve and Cartier Island Marine Reserve: Draft Management Plan*, Environment Australia, Canberra, 2001, p. 69.

9 Interview (Balint) with Tom Morris, Fisheries Western Australia, for *Troubled Waters*, Fremantle, 24 April 2001.

10 Garrett Hardin, 'The tragedy of the commons', *Science*, no. 63, 1968, pp. 1243–8.

11 Letter from Djishard Bakuama and eight others in Broome Regional Prison, West Australian, 5 April 1998.

12 Interview (Balint) with Peter Isak Husein, Johni Fakie, Tom Therik et al, Tablolong, West Timor, May 2001.

13 Jane Carruthers, 'Nationhood and national parks: Comparative examples from the post-imperial experience', in Tom Griffiths and Libby Robin (eds), *Ecology and Empire: Environmental History of Settler Societies*, Melbourne University Press, 1997, p. 127.

14 James J. Fox, op. cit., p. 135

15 Roderick Nash, *Wilderness and the American Mind*, Yale University Press, 1982, p. 270.

16 David Lowenthal, *The Past is a Foreign Country*, Cambridge University Press, 1985, p. 54.

17 Tom Griffiths, 'History and natural history: Conservation movements in conflict?', *Australian Historical Studies*, vol. 24, no. 96, 1991, p. 16.

18 *Troubled Waters*, op. cit.
19 Paul Clarke, 'Ashmore Reef: Archaeological evidence of past visitation', unpublished paper presented at the One Day Workshop on Indonesian Fishing in North Australian Waters: Questions of Utilisation and Access, Northern Territory University, Darwin, 9 March 2001, p. 5.
20 Henry Burmester, 'Island outposts of Australia', *Australia's Offshore Maritime Interests*, Occasional Papers in Maritime Affairs No. 3, Australian Centre for Maritime Studies, Canberra 1985, pp. 59–60.
21 Ibid.
22 'Ruddock to rescind secret excisions', *AM*, ABC Radio National, 18 December 2002.
23 'All at sea with boat people figures', *Sydney Morning Herald*, 16 May 2002.
24 'So far from humanity, so close to Australia', *Sydney Morning Herald*, 3–4 November 2001.
25 This photo features on the cover of Peter Mares' book, *Borderline: Australia's Treatment of Refugees and Asylum Seekers*, Reportage Series, University of New South Wales Press, 2001, although I first saw it on a billboard at the Broome office of the Australian Customs Service.

Fortress Australia

 1 This term was coined by the author of the *1987 Defence White Paper*, Paul Dibb, to describe the region to Australia's north, from East Timor through to Fiji and the Pacific. According to one newspaper article, it described the 'belt of trouble spots around [Australia's] northern approaches' ('After a long search, danger has been found', *Sydney Morning Herald*, 7 December 2000). The term became common usage in the press, eventually losing the qualifying apostrophes it originally came with. See for example, 'Paper defends our armed forces', *Canberra Times*, 9 December 2000; 'Proposed forum has role to play', *Australian Financial Review*, 11 December 2000; 'The defence story so far', *The Age*, 23 May 2001, and 'Time to rethink defence', *Courier Mail*, 7 January 2002.

2 'Our open-door borders', *The Weekend Australian*, 25–26 August 2001.

3 This information is largely taken from the findings of the *Senate Select Committee on a Certain Maritime Incident*, known as the CMI Inquiry, Parliament House, Canberra, published in October 2002 in response to the 'children overboard affair' in which government ministers were accused of lying to the public for political gain. See: http://www.aph.gov.au/senate/committee/maritime-incident-ctte/maritime/report/ contents.htm

4 Desmond Manderson, *From Mr Sin to Mr Big: A History of Australia's Drug Laws*, Oxford University Press, Melbourne, 1993, p. 17.

5 Ibid., p. 18.

6 Ibid.

7 CMI Inquiry, op. cit., chapter 1, p. 12.

8 'Troops told: Whatever it takes', *Sydney Morning Herald*, 30 August 2001.

9 Ibid., p. 6.

10 'Refugee crisis', *The Australian*, 30 August 2001. A letter was sent to the *Sydney Morning Herald* on 10 October 2001 by Mr John Faulkner, pointing out the similarities between the two men. Greg Watters also points this out in his article, 'S.S. Ocean: Dealing with boat people in the 1880s', *Australian Historical Studies*, vol. 33, no. 120, October 2002, p. 340.

11 'Hopes blown out of the water', *The Weekend Australian*, 18–19 August 2001.

12 Letter to the editor, *The Australian*, 8 November 2001.

13 Adam Graycar and Rebecca Trailby, 'People Smuggling: National Security Implications', paper prepared for the Australian Defence College, Australian Institute of Criminology, Canberra, 2000, p. 8.

14 'Defence: The looming gap', *Australian Financial Review*, 19 May 1999.

15 CMI Inquiry, op. cit., chapter 1, p. 9.

16 Ibid., chapter 2, p. 13.

17 Ibid., pp. 19–20.

18 'Secret file: Operation Relex', *Sydney Morning Herald*, 28 October 2002.

19 Letter to the CMI Inquiry from the Iraqis detained in Lombrum detention centre, Manus Island (PNG), op. cit.

20 These three statements quoted in Mungo MacCallum, 'Girt by sea: Australia, the refugees and the politics of fear', *Quarterly Essay*, 5, 2002, p. 57.

21 CMI 294–5, CMI Inquiry, op. cit., p. 36.

22 Letter to the CMI Inquiry from Iraqis detained in Lombrum detention centre, Manus Island (PNG), op. cit.

23 'Chair's Forward', CMI Inquiry, op. cit., p. xiii.

24 David Marr and Marian Wilkinson, *Dark Victory*, Allen & Unwin, Sydney, 2003, p. 160. See pp. 138–9 for an account of the *Aceng*'s arrival at Ashmore Reef.

25 CMI Inquiry, op. cit., p. 28.

26 Mungo MacCallum, op. cit., p. 86.

27 'Door is open to the people smugglers', *Sydney Morning Herald*, 12 April 1999.

28 'Air of doubt over coastal security', *The Australian*, 13 April 1999.

29 David Walker, *Anxious Nation: Australia and the Rise of Asia, 1850–1939*, University of Queensland Press, St Lucia, 1999, p. 4.

30 Graycar and Trilby, op. cit., p. 6.

31 'Smugglers swap drugs for people', *The Daily Telegraph*, 13 April 1999.

32 'Alien scam', *Herald Sun*, 13 October 1999.

33 'Smugglers are "scum of the earth"', *Sydney Morning Herald*, 30 August 2001.

34 'People smuggling linked to drugs', *The Australian*, 13 April 1999.

35 'Day trip to freedom', *Sydney Morning Herald*, 20 November 1999.

36 'When the boat comes in', *The Weekend Australian*, 17–18 April 1999.

37 'Revealed among the boat people: Mass murderers', *Sydney Morning Herald*, 16 June 2000.

38 'PM plays last boat fear card', *The Australian*, 8 November 2001.

39 Ibid.

40 Haidar al-Zoohairi's family, including his wife, two children and brother-in-law, were reported to have paid US$5000, or AUS$9926, to an organiser to come to Australia. They were among the over 350 people who perished on the *SIEV X*. See: 'For the sake of the children', *Sydney Morning Herald*, 27–28 October 2001.

41 Jonathon Hunyor, 'Don't Jail the Ferryman: The Sentencing of Indonesian "People Movers"', paper presented at the Eighth Biennial Conference of the Criminal Lawyers Association of the Northern Territory, unpublished, Darwin, 26 June 2001, p. 2.

42 Tony McInerney, from the AFP People-Smuggling team, published an article in the AFP journal, *Platypus*, acknowledging this. He is quoted in Peter Mares, *Borderline: Australia's Treatment of Refugees and Asylum Seekers*, University of New South Wales Press, Sydney, 2001, p. 188

43 Ibid.

44 See Marr and Wilkinson, op. cit., pp. 138, 148.

45 Ted Wilkinson interviewed for *AM*, ABC Radio National, 22 November 1999.

46 'Tough sentence for Indonesian people smuggler', *AM*, ABC Radio National, 20 May 2000.

47 'Pay option for people-smuggling fishermen', *Sydney Morning Herald*, 5 August 2000.

48 'Tampa people smugglers sentenced', *PM*, ABC Radio National, 27 September 2002.

49 Gaston Bachelard, quoted in Simon Schama, *Landscape and Memory*, Harper Collins, London, 1996, p. 244.

Epilogue

1 Letter to the author from Johni Fakie, no date, received January 2000.

2 Ibid.

3 Interview (Balint) with Sadli Hudari Ardani, Pepela, Rote, May 2001.

4 Letter to the author from Sadli Hudari Ardani, 17 June 2003.

5 Ibid.

6 *Troubled Waters*, Resonance Productions, 2001.

SELECT
BIBLIOGRAPHY

Aditjondro, George, *Is Oil Thicker Than Blood? A Study of Oil Companies' Interests and Western Complicity in Indonesia's Annexation of East Timor,* Nova Scotia Publishers, New York, 1999.

'Administrative Arrangements for Indonesian Fishermen Detained in Australian Waters', *Report Under S35A of the Ombudsman's Act 1976,* Canberra, August 1998.

Anderson, Warwick, *The Cultivation of Whiteness: Science, Health and Racial Destiny in Australia,* Melbourne University Press, Melbourne, 2002.

Ashmore Reef National Nature Reserve and Cartier Island Marine Reserve, Draft Management Plan, Environment Australia, Canberra, 2001.

Attwood, Bain, and Andrew Markus, *The Struggle for Aboriginal Land Rights: A Documentary History,* Allen & Unwin, Sydney, 1999.

Bach, John, *A Maritime History of Australia*, Thomas Nelson (Australia), Melbourne, 1976.

_____ 'The Pearl-shelling industry and the White Australia Policy', *Historical Studies,* vol. 10, no. 38, May 1962.

Bailey, John, *The White Divers of Broome: The True Story of a Fatal Experiment,* Pan Macmillan Australia, Sydney, 2001.

Bain, Mary Albertus, *Full Fathom Five*, Artlook Books, Perth, 1982.

Balint, Ruth, 'The last frontier: Australia's maritime territories and the policing of Indonesian fishermen', *Journal of Australian Studies*, no. 63, 2000.

_____ (writer/director) *Troubled Waters*, Resonance Productions, Sydney, 2001.

_____ (reporter) 'The Death of Mansur', *Insight*, SBS Television, 21 August 2003.

Bird Rose, Deborah, *Nourishing Terrains: Australian Aboriginal Views of Landscape and Wilderness,* Australian Heritage Commission, Canberra, 1996.

Black, Jeremy, *Maps and Politics,* University of Chicago Press, 1997.

Blackstone, William, *Commentaries on the Laws of England,* 18th edition, vol. 2, Clarendon Press, Oxford, 1979.

Barlow, Colin and Joan Hardjono (eds), *Indonesia Assessment 1995: Development in Eastern Indonesia,* Research School of Asian and Pacific Studies, Australian National University, Canberra and Singapore, 1995.

Bashford, Alison, 'Quarantine and the imagining of the Australian nation', *Health: An Interdisciplinary Journal for the Social Study of Health, Illness and Medicine,* vol. 2, no. 4, October 1998.

Brennan S. J., Frank, 'The Timor Sea oil and gas: What's fair?', *Catholic Social Justice Series,* Sydney, 2004.

Broeze, Frank, 'From the periphery to the mainstream: The challenge of Australia's maritime history', *The Great Circle*, vol. II, no. 1, 1989.

_____ *Island Nation: A History of Australians and the Sea,* Allen & Unwin, Sydney, 1998.

Brown, Anthony J., *Ill-Starred Captains: Flinders and Baudin,* Fremantle Arts Centre Press, Fremantle, 2004.

Burke, Anthony, *In Fear of Security: Australia's Invasion Anxiety,* Pluto Press, Sydney, 2001.

Burmester, Henry, 'Island outposts of Australia', in *Australia's Offshore Maritime Interests,* Occasional Papers in Maritime Affairs 3, Australian Centre for Maritime Studies, Canberra, 1985.

Burmingham, Nick, 'Unwelcome visitors at the two hundredth birthday party: A perspective on recent illegal Indonesian fishing in Australian waters', *Northern Perspective,* vol. II, no. 1, 1989.

Campbell, Bill, 'Maritime boundary arrangements in the Timor Sea', in Donald Rothwell and Martin Tsamenyi (eds), *The Maritime Dimensions of Independent East Timor,* Centre for Maritime Policy, University of Wollongong, 2000.

Campbell, Bruce C., 'The last colonial act: The expulsion of Indonesian fishermen from the northwest coast', in Jan Gothard (ed.), *Asian Orientations: Studies in Western Australian History,* no. 16, Centre for Western Australian History, University of Western Australia, 1995.

Campbell, Bruce C., and Bu V. Wilson, *The Politics of Exclusion: Indonesian Fishing in the Australian Fishing Zone,* Indian Ocean Centre for Peace Studies, no. 5, Perth, 1993.

Chi, Maxine, 'Saltwater people: Aboriginal use of sea resources, Broome, Western Australia', MA thesis, Centre for Aboriginal Studies, Curtin University of Technology, 2002.

Choo, Christine, 'Asian men on the west Kimberley coast, 1900–1940', in Jan Gothard (ed.), *Asian Orientation: Studies in Western Australian History,* no. 16, Centre for Western Australian History, University of Western Australia, 1995.

Clarke, Anne, 'The Moorman's Trowsers: Macassan and Aboriginal interactions', in Sue O'Connor and Peter Veth (eds), *East of Wallace's Line: Studies of Past and Present Maritime Cultures of the Indo-Pacific Region,* A. A. Balkema, Rotterdam, The Netherlands, 2000.

Connell, John, Phillip Hirch and Richard Howitt (eds), *Resources, Nations and Indigenous Peoples: Case Studies from Australia, Melanesia and Southeast Asia,* Oxford University Press, Melbourne, 1996.

Cordell, John (ed.), *A Sea of Small Boats,* Cultural Survival Report 26, Cultural Survival Inc., Cambridge, 1989.

Crawford, Ian, *We Won the Victory: Aborigines and Outsiders on the North-West Coast of the Kimberley,* Fremantle Arts Centre Press, Fremantle, 2001.

Crawford, John, *History of the Indian Archipalego* (1820), Frank Cass and Co, London, 1967.

Darling, John, (writer/director), *Below the Wind,* Ronin Films, Canberra, 1994.

Dening, Greg, *Performances*, Melbourne University Press, Melbourne, 1996,

De Certeau, Michel, *The Practice of Everyday Life,* University of California Press, Berkeley and Los Angeles, California, 1988.

Dwyer, Daniel, 'Fishers of people: From reef fishing to refugees, the changing role of Indonesian sailors and their *perahu* at Ashmore Reef, north Australia', in Clayton Frederickson and Ian Walters (eds), *Altered States: Material Culture Transformations in the Arafura Region,* Northern Territory University Press, Darwin, 2001.

Earl, George W., *Enterprise in Tropical Australia,* Madden and Malcolm, London, 1846.

_____ *Sailing Directions for the Arafura Sea,* Hydrographic Office, London and Sydney, 1839.

Ellis, Richard, *The Empty Ocean: Plundering the World's Marine Life,* Shearwater Books, Island Press, Washington, 2003.

Estensen, Miriam, *Matthew Flinders: The Life of Matthew Flinders,* Allen & Unwin, Sydney, 2002.

Fanon, Franz, *The Wretched of the Earth,* Penguin, London, 1965.

Fairbridge, R. W., 'Discoveries in the Timor Sea, North West Australia', *Royal Australian Historical Society Journal and Proceedings,* vol. 38, no. V, 1948.

Fegan, Brian, 'Plundering the Sea. Regulating trawling companies is difficult when the Navy is in business with them', *Inside Indonesia,* no. 73, January–March 2003.

Fenn, Percy, 'Origins of the Theory of Territorial Waters', *American Journal of International Law,* no. 20, 1926.

Flinders, Matthew, *A Voyage to Terra Australis . . . in the Years 1801, 1802 and 1803 in His Majesty's Ship the Investigator,* G. and W. Nicol, London, 1814.

Fox, James J., *Harvest of the Palm: Ecological Change in Eastern Indonesia,* Harvard University Press, Cambridge and London, 1977.

_____ 'Maritime communities in the Timor and Arafura region: Some historical and anthropological perspectives', in Sue O'Connor and Peter Veth (eds), *East of Wallace's Line: Studies of Past and Present Maritime Cultures of the Indo-Pacific Region,* A. A. Balkema, Rotterdam, The Netherlands, 2000.

_____ 'Reefs and shoals in Australia–Indonesia relations: Traditional Indonesian fishermen', in Anthony Milner and Mary Quilty (eds), *Australia in Asia. Episodes,* Oxford University Press, Melbourne, 1999.

Freycinet, L., and Peron, F., *Voyage de Decourtes aux Terres Australis,* vol. 2, Paris, 1816.

Ganter, Regina, *The Pearlshellers of Torres Strait: Resource Use, Development and Decline, 1860s–1960s,* Melbourne University Press, Melbourne, 1994.

Garran, Robert, and Don Greenlees, *Deliverance: The Inside Story of East Timor's Fight for Freedom,* Allen & Unwin, Sydney, 2002.

Goldsworthy, David (ed.), *Facing North: A Century of Australian Engagement with Asia. Volume 1: 1901 to the 1970s,* Department of Foreign Affairs and Trade, Melbourne University Press, Melbourne, 2001.

Griffiths, Tom, 'History and natural history: Conservation movements in conflict', *Australian Historical Studies,* vol. 24, no. 96, 1991.

_____ *Hunters and Collectors: The Antiquarian Imagination in Australia,* Cambridge University Press, Cambridge, 1996.

Griffiths, Tom and Libby Robin (eds), *Ecology and Empire: Environmental History of Settler Societies,* Melbourne University Press, Melbourne, 1997.

Grotius, Hugo, *The Freedom of the Seas or the Right Which Belongs to the Dutch to Take Part in the East Indian Trade,* New York, Orno Press, 1972. [First Latin edition 1633. Ruan Deman Magoffin Translation, Mare Liberum.]

Grove, Richard H., *Green Imperialism: Colonial Expansion, Tropical Island Edens and the Origins of Environmentalism 1600–1860,* Cambridge University Press, Cambridge, 1995.

Hage, Ghassan, *Against Paranoid Nationalism: Searching for Hope in a Shrinking Society,* Pluto Press Australia, Sydney, 2003.

_____ *White Nation: Fantasies of White Supremacy in a Multicultural Society,* Pluto Press Australia, Sydney, 1998.

Hamilton-Paterson, James, *The Great Deep: The Sea and its Thresholds,* Random House, New York, 1992.

Hardin, Garrett, 'The Tragedy of the Commons', *Science*, no. 63, 1968.

Harley, J. B., 'Deconstructing the Map', in Trevor Barnes and James Duncan (eds), *Writing Worlds: Discourse, Text and Metaphor in the Representation of the Landscape,* Routledge and Kegan Paul, London and New York, 1992.

_____ 'Maps, Knowledge and Power', in D. Cosgrove and S. Daniels (eds), *The Iconography of Landscape,* Cambridge University Press, Cambridge, 1988.

Hobbs, D. R., and M. J. Morwood, 'The Asian connection: Preliminary report on Indonesian trepang sites on the Kimberley coast, N.W. Australia', *Archaeology in Oceania,* no. 32, 1997.

Horridge, Adrian, *The Prahu,* Oxford University Press, London, 1981.

Hviding, Edvard, *Guardians of Marovo Lagoon,* University of Hawaii Press, Honolulu, 1996.

Jackson, Susan E., 'The water is not empty: Cross cultural issues in conceptualising sea space', *Australian Geographer,* vol. 26, no. 1, 1995.

Kaye, Stuart, *Australia's Maritime Boundaries,* Wollongong Papers on Maritime Policy no. 4, Centre for Maritime Policy, University of Wollongong, Wollongong, 1995.

Keen, Ian, 'Aboriginal Tenure and use of the foreshore and seas: An anthropological evaluation of the Northern Territory legislation providing for the closure of the seas adjacent to the land', *Anthropological Forum,* no. 5, 1984.

Kyselka, Will, *An Ocean in Mind,* Hawaii University Press, Honolulu, 1987.

La Ode Arafin and Others v. Colin William Ostle and Others, Full Court of the Supreme Court of Western Australia, no. 8923AC, 18 June 1991.

Lefebvre, Henry, *The Production of Space,* trans. Donald Nicholson-Smith, Basil Blackwell, Oxford, 1991.

Lowenthal, David, *The Past is a Foreign Country,* Cambridge University Press, Cambridge, 1985.

Lumb, Richard, D., *The Law of the Sea and Australian Off-Shore Areas,* University of Queensland Press, Brisbane, 1981.

MacCallum, Mungo, 'Girt by sea: Australia, the refugees and the politics of fear', *Quarterly Essay,* vol. 5, 2002.

MacKnight, Campbell C., *The Voyage to Marege: Macassan Trepangers in Northern Australia,* Melbourne University Press, Melbourne, 1976.

Marcus, George and Michael Fischer, *Anthropology as Cultural Critique: An Experimental Moment in the Human Sciences,* University of Chicago Press, Chicago, 1986.

Mares, Peter, *Borderline: Australia's Treatment of Refugees and Asylum Seekers,* University of New South Wales Press, Sydney, 2001.

Marr, David and Marian Wilkinson, *Dark Victory,* Allen & Unwin, Sydney, 2003.

McLoughlin, Kevin and Bruce Waller, *Review of Indonesian Fishing in the Australian Fishing Zone,* paper prepared for Fisheries

Policy Branch, Department of Primary Industries and Energy, Canberra, April 1995.

McKee, Geoffrey, 'The new Timor Gap: Will Australia now break with the past?', *Inside Indonesia,* vol. 62, April–June 2000.

Meaney, Neville, *The Search for Security in the Pacific,* Sydney University Press, Sydney, 1976.

Memmi, Albert, *The Colonized and the Coloniser,* Beacon Press, Boston, 1967.

Mellor, Jim, *Bounty Versus Boundaries: The Pursuit of Equity and Certainty Over and Down Under the Timor Sea,* unpublished report for the East Timor Centre for Independent Information on the Timor Sea, 2002.

Mitchell, Susan, 'Culture contact and indigenous economies on the Cobourg Peninsula Northwestern Arnhem Land', unpublished PhD thesis, Northern Territory University, Darwin, 1994.

North Sea Continental Shelf Cases, International Court of Jursidiction, The Hague, 1969.

Prescott, J. R. V., *Australia's Continental Shelf,* Thomas Nelson (Australia) in association with the Australian Institute of International Affairs, Melbourne, 1979.

_____ *Australia's Maritime Boundaries,* Department of International Relations, Australian National University, Canberra, 1985.

_____ *The Maritime Political Boundaries of the World,* Methuen, London and New York, 1986.

Reid, Anthony, 'Illegal entry! Indonesian fishermen detained in Broome: a report on the social and economic background', *Occasional Paper Series No. 1,* Centre for Southeast Asian Studies, Northern Territory University, Darwin, 1992.

Reynolds, Henry, *Aboriginal Sovereignty: Reflections on Race, State and Nation,* Allen & Unwin, Sydney, 1996.

_____ *The Law of the Land,* Penguin Books, Ringwood, 1987.

Rothwell, Donald, R., and Martin Tsamenyi, *The Maritime Dimensions of Independent East Timor,* Centre for Maritime Policy, University of Wollongong, 2000.

Rundle, Guy, 'The opportunist: John Howard and the triumph of reaction', *Quarterly Essay,* vol. 3, 2001.

Russell, B. C., and Vail, L. L., *Report on Traditional Indonesian Fishing Activities at Ashmore Reef Nature Reserve,* Australian National Parks and Wildlife Service, Darwin, 1988.

Said, Edward, *Orientalism,* Penguin Books, Ringwood, 1978.

Schama, Simon, *Landscape and Memory,* Fontana Press, London, 1996.

Selden, John, *Mare Clausum: The Right and Dominion of the Sea,* 2 vols, Andrew Kembe and Edward Thomas, London, 1663 [first published by Bonaventura and Abraham Elzevier in Leyden, The Netherlands, 1636].

Senate Select Committee on a Certain Maritime Incident (CMI), Parliament House, Canberra, October 2002, http://www. aph.gov.au/senate/committee/maritime-incident-ctte/maritime/report/contents.htm

Serventy, D. L., 'Indonesian fishing activity in Australian waters', *The Australian Geographer,* vol. I, no. 1, 1952.

Sharp, Nonie, *Saltwater People: The Waves of Memory,* Allen & Unwin, Sydney, 2002.

_____ 'Terrestrial and marine space in imagination and social life', *Arena Journal,* no.10, 1998.

Southon, Michael, *The Navel of the* Perahu*: Meaning and Values in the Maritime Trading Economy of a Butonese Village,* Research School of Pacific and Asian Studies, Australian National University, Canberra, 1995.

Stacey, Natasha, 'Boats to Burn. Bajo Fishing Activity in the Australian Fishing Zone', unpublished PhD thesis, Northern Territory University, Darwin, 1999.

Sutherland, Heather, 'Eastern emporium and company town: Trade and society in eighteenth century Makassar', in Frank Broeze (ed.), *Brides of the Sea: Port Cities of Asia from the 16th–20th Centuries,* New South Wales University Press, Sydney, 1989.

The Commonwealth v. Yarmirr; Yarmirr v. Northern Territory (2001), High Court of Australia, 56, 11 October 2001.

The Law of the Sea: United Nations Convention on the Law of the Sea, United Nations, New York, 1983.

The Law Reform Commission, *The Recognition of Aboriginal Customary Laws,* vol. 2, report no. 31, Australian Publishing Service, Canberra, 1986.

Tiffen, Rodney, *Diplomatic Deceits: Government, Media and East Timor,* University of New South Wales Press, Sydney, 2001.

Torgovnick, Marianna, *Gone Primitive: Savage Intellects, Modern Lives,* University of Chicago Press, Chicago and London, 1990.

Walker, David, *Anxious Nation: Australia and the Rise of Asia, 1850-1939,* University of Queensland Press, Brisbane, 1999.

_____ 'Survivalist anxieties: Australian responses to Asia, 1980s to the present', *Australian Historical Studies*, vol. 33, no. 120, October 2002.

Wallace, Alfred R., *The Malay Archipelago: The Land of the Orang-Utan and the Birds of Paradise. A Narrative of Travel with Studies of Man and Nature, 1869*, Oxford University Press, Oxford, 1986.

Winichakul, Thongchai, *Siam Mapped: The History of the Geo-Body of a Nation,* University of Hawaii Press, Honolulu, 1994.

Wood, Denis, *The Power of Maps,* Guilford Press, New York, 1992.

Urry, J., and M. Walsh, 'The lost "Macassar language" of northern Australia', *Aboriginal History,* no. 5, 1981.

INDEX